September Monkey

September Monkey

INDUK PAHK

Harper & Brothers, New York

SEPTEMBER MONKEY

Library of Congress catalogue card number: 54-8981

To Velma Jeanette Van Court
who has opened her heart and home to me
in the warm and loving manner
which makes so many turn to her for
love and strength

Contents

Foreword

My object in writing this book has been first to witness what can happen in a life when the power of God grips a heart, mind and soul. My mother was a village woman born in the days when the weighty traditions and conventions accumulated throughout the centuries had become especially burdensome. Christianity acted as a lever and fulcrum to dislodge her from the stony soil of the past and to lift her above tragedy, fear and superstition. It also brought the living water which made the soil fertile again. And in this new soil I was rooted and nourished.

My second aim in writing this story is to express my gratitude to my friends who have contributed so much that is endearing and broadening and inspirational to my life on two continents. In my heart Koreans and Americans are all one family; indeed, my experiences in many parts of the world have made me aware of the sweet kinship of all peoples.

Particularly I wish to express my sincere gratitude to Mrs. Elwood S. DuBois of Salem, New Jersey, to Mrs. William F. Becker, sister of Miss Velma Jeanette Van Court with whom I make my home.

INDUK PAHK

Wainwright House
Rye, New York
July 27, 1954

September Monkey

I

Introducing September Monkey

The scene was set in a small village of Monyangtul, three miles directly west of the port town of Chinnampo in North Korea. As a September dawn ushered in a new day an infant cry announced the arrival of another member of the Pahk family. Here, in a modest thatch-roofed house, an illiterate Buddhist mother and a scholarly Confucian father had eagerly awaited the birth of their fourth child, whom they desperately hoped would be a son and heir. Three times before they had waited thus and each time a boy had been born only to die in infancy, leaving them desolate and lonely. According to Confucian standards a family must have a boy to continue the family name, to worship the ancestors and to inherit the family property. Therefore, in the beginning I was a great disappointment to my parents. My father's ultimate reaction, however, was favorable.

"Well, she's better than nothing. The main question is whether or not she will live!"

Being a scholar, Father was able to look into the future of this new girl-child by the ancient Oriental signs. Finding that I was born in the year of the monkey, the month of the rooster, the day of the dragon and the hour of the tiger, he complained,

"If only this baby were a boy, what a great career he would have! As it is she will lead an extraordinary life."

Mother smiled to herself. "Since this is the year of the monkey, she is a September monkey and she will be very clever." And so they laughed together and were reconciled to me.

In Korea great care is taken in choosing a good name for the newborn child as one's name is as important as one's face. When a child does wrong the parent says, "I cannot show my face," and from this reaction comes the Oriental expression "losing face." Also we say to a child, "You must live up to your name."

In view of the strong animal signs under which I was born, Father pondered long and carefully concerning a proper name for me. He said, "She is a monkey, a rooster, a dragon and a tiger. What if she shows all these natures—acting like a monkey, crowing like a rooster, powerful as a dragon and raging like a tiger? A boy with these endowments might stir the world! It is too bad she is a girl for if she behaves according to her signs, I shall surely lose face."

In order to counteract all these strong traits he decided to give me a good feminine name, so he called me "Im-duk," which means "virtuous woman." The first syllable, "Im," comes from the name of the mother of a famous Chinese emperor and by giving me this name he expected me to be like my illustrious model. In Korea, in order to be considered virtuous, a woman must be quiet, obedient, gentle and devoted.

Korean parents always select Chinese characters for names because Chinese culture is our mother culture; the Chinese language is an older literary language and was long used by Korean scholars before the Korean vernacular became a written language. For boys, characters signifying heroism, power, success and bravery are popular, or those designating strong character such as rock, tiger or dragon, or characters signifying long life, such as the turtle and the pine tree. For girls, the names of flowers, jewels or some virtue are preferable—"beautiful as flowers," "precious as jewels" or "virtuous as an angel." Sometimes girls are given boys' names as they are in certain American families.

When a male child reaches maturity and is ready to be married and take his place in society, he may then be given another name by his family, denoting their aspiration for him. But also he may choose a pen name for himself, signifying his own professional ambition. Then such names as "flying tiger," "morning star," "spring garden," "autumn lake" and "lone pine" are preferred. I also chose a pen name at one time—Myong-Jong, which means "pealing bell." I liked its onomatopoeic sound, and I wished my message to ring out.

In some instances the daughter of a well-known family is given a new legal name when she enters her husband's family and this name is used for registration purposes while she still retains her own family name. For example, Kim Chin-Ju married into the Lee family and registered into that family as the wife of Lee Young-Ho, while her family would still refer to her as "Kim Chin-Ju, the house of Lee." In introducing this couple the person making the introduction would say, "This is Mrs. Kim Chin-Ju, wife of Mr. Lee Young-Ho," or "This is Mr. Lee Young-Ho, husband of Mrs. Kim Chin-Ju." In this way the person to whom they are introduced will know instantly the family connections of the lady. The children take the father's name, such as "This is Lee Chung-Sik, son of Lee Young-Ho," or, the mother's name may also be included. When the mother is well known her name is usually given. Today if the husband is prominent the wife is merely introduced as Madame or Mrs. Lee, or whatever the husband's name may be.

Since two Chinese syllables are usually used to make a given name, brothers and sisters are frequently given one syllable in common and in this way brothers and sisters can be identified as such. For example, Young-Sook and In-Sook for sisters; Dong-Sun and Dong-Suk for brothers; and Dong-Sun and Dong-Hee for brother and sister. The character of Sun signifies boy while Hee signifies girl.

And so I, being a September monkey, was named Imduk, in an effort to offset all the unwomanly traits which my animal signs indicated.

In order to round out a discussion of names, my parents too had names of striking significance. Father's name was Young-Ha, meaning Eternal Stream, while Mother's name was Kim Onyu, meaning Meek. No doubt my maternal grandparents hoped to imbue their child with a quality which her animal signs did not portend, since Mother's nature was anything but meek.

Six years passed, during which time a little brother came into our family. Then an epidemic of cholera swept the village where we lived and in two months' time two-thirds of the people died. The Pahk family alone lost six immediate relatives, including my father and little brother. Great devotion was displayed by the women at this crucial time, my aunt having cut off the tip of her left ring finger in order to drop her lifeblood into the mouth of her dying husband. I was fortunate to escape the cholera but having suffered a series of childhood diseases in my brief six years of life, I was so weak and sickly that nobody thought I would live.

After the death of my father and brother, the relatives assembled, headed by my great-uncle, to decide what to do about the inheritance After much deliberation their decision was presented to my mother. "We have chosen a boy from the family of the nearest relative to be the heir of the deceased. Take him as your son and heir."

This ultimatum meant that Mother would have to be sub-servient to the new-chosen heir and that behind him would be his father acting as regent to our family. Knowing that she would be dependent on this boy and his family and that she would have no rights over the estate or family affairs, my poor bereaved mother was beside herself with anxiety as to what she should do. She felt she simply could not accept the family decision but she knew no way to reject it. So she prayed to Buddha, the only god she knew.

"Man's extremity is God's opportunity"—and just when the way looked blackest, Mother's cousin, a devout Christian who was later stoned to death for his faith, called on her to comfort her. In her anguish Mother cried, "What can I do? Where shall I go?"

He said, "There is one great exit."

This good news was like an electric shock to Mother, and she begged, "Where is it? Tell me quickly, I am ready to leave at any time. I have lost all. There is nothing more to lose and everything to gain if I can only find my way."

Gently he told her, "Jesus Christ is the way, the truth, and the life. If you follow him, he will take you into a new life, for his Father—our Father—God, the Father, is love."

Love, love, that is what she needed—love and understanding. Scarcely able to believe it she said, "Do you mean to say that God is my father?" Buddha had never had such a personal meaning to her as that.

Again her cousin reassured her, "Yes, God is your Father, and He knows that you have no son but that if you educate your daughter she can take the place of a son."

Hope stirred within her. "How do you know that God loves me? Where can I find Him?"

Then he explained to her the basic tenets of Christianity of which he himself was so sure. "Come along," he concluded, "I will tell you where you can find him." Then Cousin Kim told my perplexed mother of the Christian church three miles away in Chinnampo where she might hear the story of this Jesus and she promised to meet him there later in the day. It happened to be Christmas Day. We walked down the snowy desolate road, a lonely, heartbroken village woman holding a little girl by the hand, seeking the new way of life. I still remember that my mother wore the white of mourning—long skirt over her long trousers and short jacket, with kerchief round her head to ward off the cold, while I wore long black trousers, pink skirt and yellow blouse all padded in winter fashion. On our feet were straw shoes, but our white stockings were padded. When we arrived at the church a handful of native converts were singing songs. I thought the singing was very beautiful. As the service went on my mother was comforted and reassured by the simple message about the Christ Child who came to save the people from their sins and mistakes and to help them live their days in service, love and joy. That day Mother learned that the meaning of the name JESUS is "to save from sin" and that the Jewish people, like the Korean people, gave good names to their children to influence them for good.

At the end of the service Christmas gifts were distributed to the children, and I was given a yellow writing pad and yellow pencil No. 2. This pad and yellow pencil were the most beautiful gifts I had ever received and I shall never forget the magical number "2" which was inscribed on the pencil.

Encouraged by the wonderful message of Christ's love and the beautiful gift given to her little girl, my mother wholeheartedly accepted the new way of life and her name was added to the church roll. As we walked homeward, I, clutching the precious yellow pencil and pad and Mother holding close to her heart the new hope she had found in Christ—the vision of her little girl learning to read and write just like a boy—she made her second big decision. "You are not going to waste that pad and pencil; you are going to use it in learning to read and write!"

Being a woman of strong determination, the very next day Mother secured an old village man to teach me the Korean phonetic alphabet. This alphabet is composed of 140 phonetic symbols formed from 24 characters and is so marvelously simple and regular in design that a reasonably intelligent person finds it no hard task to learn it in a day or so. It is considered by experts to be the most nearly perfect phonetic system ever devised. Almost any sound may be reproduced with it. This alphabet had been devised in the fifteenth century partly as an intellectual revolt against Chinese influence in general and against the intricate Chinese characters and classics in particular. Compared to Chinese writing it was so simple that the scholars had derisively cried, "It is too easy, except for women and girls." In the intervening years this alphabet, called Hangul, had been almost forgotten until the Christian missionaries arrived in the early eighties and began to seek a simplified means of teaching the common people. In this phonetic system they discovered a wonderful implement of learning. However, no real national progress was possible until 1945 when Korea was liberated from Japan, and it was officially decided to use the phonetic alphabet for teaching in the schools.

This alphabet was conquered in two weeks with the aid of the little yellow pad and the yellow pencil No. 2. Since learning the alphabet was the test of my ability to learn at all, Mother jumped a foot in the air for joy, as she cried, "She has brains! She has brains! Surely this child is showing signs of becoming a September monkey! I must give her more education—but when, where and how, with no schools for girls hereabouts?"

There were schools for girls which had been founded by different missions but they were too far away. No transportation was available, there was no money, and I was too young for boarding school.

Faithfully Mother and I attended church services every Sunday while family gossip passed from one mouth to another concerning how terrible it was for a young widow and her child to go into a strange group, mixing with unknown people, both men and women. Under pressure of this gossip the family finally decided to ostracize us unless Mother were willing to give up this new life. She must choose between the old and the new, between the adopted son within the conventional setup approved by her family and her stubborn, strange new ways. Boldly my mother decided to leave the

Pahk family and to move to her youngest brother's home where she could follow the new adventure. Because she was unwilling to accept the heir chosen for her by her husband's family, the estate was divided among the male relatives. Mother was given fifteen dollars and was left unfettered by all family ties. She was free! "Know the truth, and the truth shall make you free" had already become the living Word to her.

2

A Girl-Boy

All the earthly possessions Mother had were the fifteen dollars, a bundle of clothing, and me with the yellow pad and pencil. Looking into the future with a great faith in her new God, her Father's love, she started out for her new life. We walked all afternoon over the lonely country road until sunset when we arrived at her youngest brother's home in Sanmock, seven miles northwest of Monyangtul. My uncle was a widower, his wife having only recently died, leaving two motherless little girls—one two years older and one two years younger than I.

When Mother told her brother, Kim Yong-Ho, that she had accepted the new religion and had decided to educate me, he was violently angry and shouted, "What do you think she is going to be? Why do you think she will ever learn?"

With great assurance Mother replied, "She has already proved her ability to learn. She can read and write."

Then as he looked on with unbelieving eyes, I took out my yellow pad and yellow pencil No. 2 and wrote the phonetic alphabet. Completely disarmed by my performance, he muttered, "But there is no school for girls."

Being without a wife, having little property, and with a sister and her child newly accepted as responsibilities, my uncle began to get drunk on rice wine. He came home every night intoxicated and quarreled with Mother about her acceptance of the new religion and her decision to educate her daughter. Angrily he chided her for her stubbornness and determination in times past, such as the time she had insisted upon taking her pet dog with her to her new home when she was married. Mother always loved dogs. She kept one or two dogs all through her life from childhood until she died at the age of eighty-five. At the time she was married she had a brown dog belonging to the beagle family. She called her dog Bok-Suree, meaning Blessed Dog. Mother took her to the wells where she drew water, to the fields where she hoed and picked cotton. They were inseparable friends. When her wedding day approached Mother made only one request—to have permission to take Bok-Suree along when she would go to her new home. Of course her mother flatly said "No." The idea of a bride taking a pet dog to her husband's home was incredible because the majority of Koreans would never keep a dog as a pet. It was then customary for the bride and groom to spend the first two nights after their wedding at the bride's home. When the time came for my mother to leave her old home, her family had a hard time to keep Bok-Suree from following her sedan chair. Toward suppertime on the day after her arrival at her new home a strange brown dog was seen prowling round and round the house. The December day was gray and cold; the dog looked weary and pitiful. My paternal grandmother let her come into the kitchen to have something to eat. Mother was busy getting the first meal in her new home. There

Bok-Suree and Mother met! Bok-Suree leaped for joy, whimpering and panting and licking Mother, while Mother petted her and wept. Loyal Bok-Suree! She had searched diligently along a ten-mile stretch of strange territory in order to be reunited with her beloved mistress. Without any question my paternal grandmother kept Bok-Suree which was a great relief to my maternal grandmother.

Each night Uncle would storm through the past, berate the present and scorn the future. "Never has anyone in our family had such wild ideas before! Where do you expect to get the money for all of this education?"

Quietly and prayerfully, while he continued to persecute her, Mother made her plans. After days and weeks of careful thinking and recalling stories she had heard in the past, she came up with a wonderful idea. There was one story of a young, handsome Chinese girl who put on a soldier's uniform and went to war. After a while she fell in love with her general and they were married. Mother used to tell me this story with many glamorous details and I thrilled to it and felt as if I were the young woman soldier. My mother's new idea was: Why not disguise Imduk as a boy and send her to the near-by boys' school in Dukdong where a distant relative, Kim Sung-No, was headmaster? At that time I was seven.

Again taking her fifteen dollars, her little bundle and me, her delicate child, she moved to the village where the boys' school was situated, got a room close to the home of her relative, the headmaster, and with his co-operation began to set her plans into motion. Dressing me in a boy's pink jacket and a pair of black trousers made out of her skirt, and changing my red ribbon to a black ribbon braided and tied into the hair just as all other little village boys wore their hair, she made me look like the boys with whom I would go to school. Then she changed my name Imduk to "Induk," a boy's name meaning "benevolence and virtue."

Taking her new girl-son by the hand, Mother led me to the one-room village school and said, "You are my son now. Remember your name. If you have been a good boy at school I will give you all the chicken gizzards you want when you come home." Knowing how much I enjoyed gizzards, she had regretted many times that when my brother was living she had given him all the gizzards. Now she would make amends.

As Mother turned away toward home, I went alone into the schoolroom where fifteen boys aged six to ten sat on the floor, cross-legged, each with a Chinese book in his hands reading aloud in a singsong fashion, swaying to and fro. They all stared at me as the teacher called me to sit at the end of the row and gave me a book entitled *One Thousand Characters*. From this book I was to learn the first eight characters that first day. Instead of eight, I learned sixteen. The next day I was required to recite and also write these sixteen characters without the textbook. Twice a month, the fifteenth and the last day, every student was required to recite all he had learned in the preceding fifteen days, and prizes were awarded, one for the pupil who learned the most and one for the pupil who recited the loudest. Being the little girl-boy born under the sign of the rooster, I got the prize for reciting the loudest. When lessons were not properly learned, the boys were whipped across the legs with sticks before the entire class. If failures were repeated, the number of times the student was struck was increased. Never was

I punished for failing to learn my lessons and I won the
prize over and over for reciting the loudest. In three months
the one thousand Chinese characters had been mastered by
reading, writing and reciting them from memory.

There is a long history behind the use of Chinese characters
in Korea. We Koreans had only a spoken language until
we began to adopt Chinese characters in the first century
A.D. They are idiographs, each having its special sound and
meaning. For example, the character for man (人) looks like
a walking pose of a man. The character for good (好) is made
up of two characters, the left one (女) is the character for
woman and the other on the right (子) is for son. A woman
with a son means "good." These are very simple examples
but there are thousands of highly complicated characters.
And each one must be learned separately, how to read it,
write it and interpret it, because it is not possible to guess
from looking at a character how it may be pronounced or
what it may mean. However, once the Chinese written
language is learned then one can converse on paper with
the literate people of Korea, China, Japan, Manchuria, Mongolia, French Indo-China and other parts of Chinese Asia.
In Southeast Asia, including Formosa, the Philippines, Malaya
and Indonesia, there are some twenty million overseas Chinese
among whom the Chinese written language is also coin of
the realm. The best writing is done with a brush and a
cake of dried ink, moistened as needed. Fine calligraphy is
as much of an art as fine painting and just as carefully
studied and respected. Obviously, this sort of learning re-
quires concentration, skill, time, money and energy. My
mother had assigned me quite an order when she maneuvered
me into the boys' school.

I joined the boys in their games which included flying kites, making willow whistles and gathering birds' eggs from the thatched roofs in the spring; climbing trees, swinging on rope swings, playing hide-and-seek and various other games during summer; spinning tops and skating in the winter. When the boys went fishing or swimming I stayed at home, lest they learn that I was a girl. However, I competed and quarreled with the best of them.

Because money was so scarce, tuition was usually paid in rice or wood. Each student helped to supply the wood for heating the classroom. The mud and stone floors which were covered with oiled paper were heated by flues running under the floor from the kitchen fireplace to the chimney. In summer these flues cooled the floors while the cooking was done in an outdoor fireplace. Today modern architects use this principle in heating and air-conditioning units. Our classroom was part of the teacher's home.

In old Korea education was motivated by the desire to obtain the highest positions in the government, which meant power, wealth and fame. Literary men were employed in key government positions so that when the king needed a man for a very important position the candidates were the talented students who had gone all the way up the school system, from village schools to district schools and from district schools to the provincial schools sponsored by the governor of the province. Each spring and fall the governor held examinations and from the successful students he chose candidates for the National Examinations held in Seoul at the highest and greatest Confucian institution, maintained under the supervision of the king himself. Not only the recommended candidates but any qualified scholar could take the National Examinations. When a candidate passed the National Examinations with highest honors he could become a governor, prime minister, minister of education or finance, and the like. Thus he might suddenly have thrust upon him all the glory man can dream of. His success was an honor to his ancestors and also to the unborn generations.

This system of education called forth extreme effort on the part of the students. Most males of old Korea did their best to get an education. Some tightened their belts to control dire hunger; some tied their long hair to overhead beams so that if they fell asleep while studying their hair would be pulled; others went out into the cold winter storms to be invigorated when they became overweary. Parents and young wives also co-operated and made every effort to help their studious sons and husbands win scholastic honors.

My grandfather had had five daughters and no son, so when his only son was born he planted two trees in the front yard in the hope that his son would grow up and pass the National Examinations after which the community would hold a celebration and my grandfather would be able to sit and watch the professional tightrope walkers who would fasten their rope to the two trees. My grandmother also had done her part, offering prayers to her god for her son's success. She said prayers every morning facing the east as she had heard that the capital where the examinations were held lay in that direction. My father had great hope for himself and three times he walked the distance of 180 miles to Seoul to take these examinations. However, during the course of years this examination system had become corrupted by bribery, and not being willing to compete in bribery each time he returned to his village filled with disappointment. Nevertheless he became a teacher and leader in the community.

Later the National Examinations were abolished but the village schools continued and it was one of these lower schools which I attended. During this year Mother also started to learn to read and write, using the Korean phonetic alphabet, meanwhile earning her living by weaving. She was an expert weaver, having been trained when a small child of eleven at which time she wove a cotton strip fourteen inches wide and ten yards long. My grandfather had taken this cloth to market, crying, "This cloth was woven by a child of eleven," and when people disbelieved him he shouted, "Come and see for yourself." Mother also raised silkworms, spun the threads and wove exquisite silk fabrics.

By the time I was eight years old she knew I would not be able to continue indefinitely to attend school disguised as a boy. Day and night she pondered and prayed for God's guidance. Again God provided an answer in the form of news that missionaries had started a girls' school in the port town of Chinnampo. This was her answer. She would change her son back to a girl by exchanging boys' clothes for girls' clothes and braiding her hair with a red ribbon. Always a woman of strong determination and action, Mother and her girl-son were ready to begin another adventure.

3

A Boy-Girl

In a sense the drastic change taking place in my life was a reflection of the changes occurring in my country, in the neighboring nations, and in the whole world at that particular time. My birth, the deaths of my father and of my only brother, the courageous decision of my mother to renounce Buddhism and accept Christianity, and to educate me besides, all came about between the two wars fought over Korea, the Sino-Japanese War of 1894-95 and the Russo-Japanese War of 1904-5.

Korea, like many other countries in Asia, had been an absolute monarchy, having some wise and strong kings as well as some unenlightened and weak ones. During the Silla dynasty there had also been two queens who ruled in their own right and never married. Their reigns were recorded in history with praise and gratitude for their wisdom and justice. Under the regime of one of these queens the astronomical observatory was built in Kyongju. It is considered the oldest existing observatory in the Far East.

In the early days the only country with which Korea had any diplomatic contact was China. Once a year we sent an ambassador with gifts to the Chinese court in Peking and he usually brought home more presents from the Chinese emperor than we had sent. To other countries Korea's door was bolted tight. No wonder she was known as a "Hermit Kingdom."

The closed door of our isolated Korea was opened for the first time in the latter part of the nineteenth century. In 1876 the Treaty of Amity, Friendship, Commerce and Navigation was signed with Japan; in 1882 the Treaty of Amity and Commerce was signed with the United States of America; and with other nations in the years following. The United States was the first Western power to which Korea accorded access.

Naturally, the newly opened door of this Hermit Kingdom attracted the zeal and enthusiasm of the Protestant churches in America and in no time the first missionaries arrived and religious works were started. A new world was set before them to conquer for Christ. Some fifty years earlier the first French Catholic missionaries had entered Korea clandestinely but were more or less persecuted by the Koreans, partly because of their ban on ancestor worship and partly because of their illegal entry. Some sixty years prior to the entry of the French priests, however, a young Korean scholar who followed his father with the Korean embassy to Peking, brought home some Catholic literature and studied it with his friends. Actually that was how Catholicism started in Korea. And so by the time the French Catholic missionaries came along there was already some degree of persecution being felt.

In 1884, two years after the treaty with the United States, there was an uprising in Seoul staged by the Progressive party leaders but instigated by the Japanese. These leaders were determined to initiate a reform, patterned after the Meiji reformation of Japan, by introducing the Western ways of life. But the Korean court, which continued to believe in China's strength, power and culture, sent a secret request for help to the Chinese premier and adviser to the emperor, Yuan Shih-kai. Thereupon Chinese soldiers, led by Yuan, came and dispersed the Progressive leaders who fled to the Japanese legation for protection. No doubt the intentions of the reformers were good but they played into the hands of their Japanese sponsors who themselves had colossal ambition toward the conquest of all of Asia. Within a decade the repulsed Japanese instigators had reinforced their strength and returned to fight the Sino-Japanese War of 1894-95, which was fought on the Korean mainland. This time Japan won over China and as a result gained Formosa and the Pescadores and forced China to recognize the independence of Korea. Thus ended the age-old role of China's power in the Far East, including her dominance over Korea. (The entry of China into the recent conflict was no isolated procedure but a continuance of an old policy of acting as arbiter of Korea's fate.)

About the turn of the century the Korean Government announced certain reforms, such as the cutting off of the long braided hair worn by boys and the topknots which had been the symbol of married men. Immediately some of the progressive young men cut their hair in the Western manner without the consent of their elders. The family commotion caused by such action is too involved to describe here. The most difficult thing in Oriental life is to break away from old traditions. Around the same time the Korean Government broke another precedent and gave a valuable gold mine concession in North Korea to an American syndicate.

After her victory over China in 1895, Japan again tried to control Korea but the king and queen and ministers, who favored China, would not permit it. Suddenly in the fall of 1895, at four o'clock in the morning of October 8, Queen Min was murdered and her body burned in Kyongbok Palace in Seoul, part of a plot staged by the Japanese in Korea. It was common knowledge that the queen held a rod of iron over the king's head, but the king tricked the Japanese out of their triumph by escaping to the Russian legation with his son, the crown prince, his scepter and his seal, and from the legation he ruled the country over a year. Thereafter Russian influence became paramount in Korea and Russia made a secret agreement concerning the fine harbor of Masanpo. In order to block Russia's domination of the Far East the Anglo-Japanese Alliance was consummated, guaranteeing the independence of Korea and the integrity of China. At the beginning of the century the reigns of Queen Victoria of Great Britain and the Empress Dowager Tzu Hsi of China were nearing a close and the bright day of royalty was overcast, although at that time few recognized the cyclonic nature of the clouds.

In February, 1904, Japan started an undeclared war on Russia, forcing the Korean Government to give every assistance possible. Much to the surprise of the rest of the world, Japan jujitsued the Russian giant out of the ring and part of the "take" was the territory of Southern Sakhalin (Karafuto) and Russia's port and rail rights in Manchuria. Thus Russia had to cease operations in Korea, as China had been forced to withdraw a decade before, and Japan's road to the conquest was freed of its major obstacles. Japanese determination in that direction had a long history, for as early as 1592 the islanders had first invaded Korea under Hideyoshi but the famous Korean Admiral Yi Sun-Syn had counterattacked with iron-clad ships and defeated the Japanese. It took three major attempts to dominate Korea but the third attempt succeeded.

While my country's fate was at stake, the Spanish-American

War of 1898 was also being fought and the United States acquired the Philippines, Puerto Rico and Guam. In 1899 Dutch resistance to the British Government in South Africa set off the Boer War. In 1900 the Chinese staged their Boxer Rebellion against all the foreign powers. This was the newly awakening, transitional and revolutionary period into which I was born. To my mother it was a most opportune time because her many questions regarding life were the very questions which depressed peoples everywhere were bringing to the fore. From her girlhood she had asked why she could not learn as her brothers did, why a woman had no property rights since she could produce as well as a man, and why her sex was treated unfairly. No one had ever been able to give her an adequate answer. For her an answer came when she embraced Christianity, for Jesus Christ whom she accepted without reservation represented the new way of life to her. In him she was free and for him she became courageous. She wanted me to know him personally as she did. She was therefore determined to take me to a school where I could learn of him while I was also acquiring an education, and so she decided that I was to go to Samsung Methodist Mission School for Girls in Chinnampo, just seven miles from the boys' school I had attended.

Needing a place to live while earning a living, my anxious mother secured a position as cook in the home of a wealthy concubine about one mile from the girls' school. Her mistress played all night and slept very late in the morning, with breakfast about eleven. That meant that I could not have fresh rice for my breakfast because the mistress must eat first and mother and daughter eat the leftovers. Therefore Mother would put away the leftover rice of the night before and warm it to give me a breakfast, since I had to walk a mile to school each day.

After about ten days of this sort of life, Mother said, "I am not going to give my son-girl the leftover rice from a concubine's table. I will go out and earn our way by other means." She asked me if I could cook my own rice. Actually she decided for me by announcing before I could make any comment, "From this day on you must cook your own rice. We are not going to waste time and energy by being one another's servant."

She decided to become a peddler while I studied. Securing a room in the school where I could sleep, she bought me a cooking kettle, a few dishes, chopsticks and a spoon, and with these utensils and an abandoned kerosene can as a stove, I was required to cook my rice in the courtyard during summer and in the schoolteacher's kitchen in the winter. The first time I tried to prepare rice I discovered that too much fire burned it; the second attempt proved that too little fire left it sadly underdone; the third time I tried it, the rice was just right.

After establishing me in school, Mother prepared a bundle of silk cloth for making children's jackets, buttons, thread, needles, embroidery silks, dyes, face-powder cakes, hair ribbons, coin purses and such. She carried this heavy burden on her back and visited from house to house, exchanging her wares for raw cotton, which she wove into more cloth in winter when she could not travel. She covered an area of about twenty miles west of Chinnampo, making her brother's home her headquarters. The cloth she wove in winter was sold in the markets conducted in the larger towns every five days. As a rule villages are nested in the valleys, and as my mother sat and rested on some hilltop overlooking the clustered homes, she always prayed, "Dear God, lead me into the homes where I can sell, for the sake of my little girl." Sometimes she wept as she prayed. Not always able to sell, she often wept for disappointment but also because she felt that her daughter was just as important as somebody else's ten sons.

Amazingly my mother, though constantly busy providing a living for us, found the time to study. And when I graduated from the girls' school Mother had by that time conquered the phonetic alphabet. She always attacked a situation by direct action and led by example.

Loneliness for my mother, who had thus far been my inseparable companion, so overcame me one day that I walked four miles to the village where I knew she was staying. But Mother, who had sacrificed so much and was trying so desperately to provide a way to give me an education, knew that she must not spoil me by affection and so she turned her back and would not receive me, saying, "I am doing my best to provide for you and you must do your part by applying yourself to your studies. God can help us through loneliness to be better workers in His Kingdom. It is also our patrotic duty to Korea." The Kingdom of Heaven and Korea's new day were much the same to her. Needless to say I returned in tears to my books, my solitary room and my little rice kettle.

Samsung School for Girls had an enrollment of about twenty students with two teachers, a woman, Isabel Chang, who acted as principal, and a man, Lee Kun-Wo, who taught the Chinese characters. The main subject was the Four Gospels, the method of study being to memorize silently, then recite aloud in oral examination. It was here that I first became familiar with the wonderful words of life which became my spiritual food as the years went by.

To me arithmetic was a new subject. Singing too was a part of the curriculum and this vocalization afforded me an opportunity such as I had never known before to give vent to pent-up feelings. The little reed organ used for accompaniment was the first such musical instrument I had ever seen. Sharps and flats were difficult for me, as Korean music has nothing of the sort. Harmonizing also intrigued me as there is no harmony in Korean music.

The study of Chinese was continued with a mixed script made up of the Korean phonetic alphabet combined with Chinese characters. In a textbook written in this mixed script I read the story of the discovery of America by Christopher Columbus in 1492, how the kings of Britain and Italy had refused to give him aid, but how friendly Isabella, queen of Spain, had given him the assistance which finally brought success. Columbus thanked the queen for her benevolence and virtue. I was thrilled beyond words to see the same Chinese characters which make up my name "Induk," meaning "benevolence" and "virtue," appearing in my textbook, used to describe the queen.

About the same time a tall, handsome young Korean came to address us and the things he told seemed unbelievable. "I have come from Hawaii, where there is no winter but spring all the year around. It is an island of flowers, surrounded by the blue waters of the Pacific, the largest ocean in the world. There are no fences, yet no one takes another's property. In this paradise there are no tropical fruits which we do not have; bananas from which you can pull the skin and place in your mouth and the delicious bite simply melts; pineapples the size of a Korean round pillow, which are so palatable that when you take a bite you would not even know whether the person opposite you is alive or dead." After he had stirred us all to go to Hawaii he closed with two proverbs, "Where there's a will there's a way" and "Heaven helps those who help themselves." That very day I made a vow to myself that someday I would travel to this paradise and perhaps even to other enchanting places of the world.

Contests in reciting the Four Gospels were conducted regularly by the minister of the local church and attended by the congregation. The minister would call the contestants to sit in the front row, then opening his Bible at random he would read a verse from the Gospels and the contestants must continue reciting from the point he left off. After receiving a prize which I shall never forget—ten sheets of fine Korean writing paper, a Chinese writing brush and a cake of black ink—I resolved to cultivate my memory in every possible way and to this end decided to memorize the Epistles and other parts of the New Testament. Was there not something symbolic in the fact that the prizes I won usually consisted of writing materials?

During the Korean New Year season, seesaw was a very popular form of recreation. Not only at the schools but all over Korea seesaw was considered a great sport for young girls and women. The length of the two halves of the board was regulated according to the weight of the girls who stood on their respective places and alternated in jumping as high into the air as possible and then landing back on the board. Swinging was also very popular, with the swinger either sitting, standing or hanging over the swing board. In the old Korea, and to some extent today, boys and girls and men and women were segregated in social life unless very closely related. When I was young high-class girls and young married women were not allowed to be seen in public unchaperoned or with faces uncovered. But youth is youth everywhere and there was a natural desire to know what those of the opposite sex were doing. So the story is that with the high swing in the back yard within the court, the girls were able to swing high enough to see the boys passing by outside. The higher the swing, the more to be seen.

In summer girls and young married women gathered a flower called *Pong Sun Wha,* pressed the juice from the blooms and leaves and mixed it with a certain sour powder, painted the finger and toenails with this mixture, wrapped green leaves around them, left them overnight, and in the morning found them stained a beautiful bright red. This process would be repeated several times and the girls vied with one another to see who was able to get the reddest nails. According to the rules, young married women painted only the last two fingers; older women painted only the little finger; but girls were entitled to paint all but the index finger and also the big toenail.

No games were played by mixed groups and even in church and Sunday School boys and girls were separated by a curtain. However, coming out of church the boys and girls saw each other and how shocked the parents were when they saw their daughters looking at the boys! One Monday morning when I was eleven years old one of my classmates quietly handed me a letter, explaining that "somebody" had sent it. On opening it I found it was from her brother who attended the boys' school and also the church Sunday School. In it he told me how much he loved me and how he would rather have me for his future wife than any other. Angry, and feeling disgraced, I sewed the letter into the lining of my jacket, hoping to find an opportunity to return it to him. One day as I was coming down the steps of the church I met him coming up. Jerking the letter from the lining of my jacket, I handed it to him, saying, "This is your letter, isn't it? Don't ever do it again."

The boy blushed and stammered and the romance was ended. (Years later I was chosen from among the teachers at Ewha to play the wedding march for this young man's marriage ceremony.)

During the spring and fall the students used to go to Pyongyang, the biggest city in the area where the largest Christian church was located, for a special two-week Bible study course taught by the missionaries at the Bible Institute. Mother and I, with other students and their mothers, walked forty miles each way to attend these classes. In addition to Bible study, talks on hygiene, sanitation and general health training were given. One of the lectures was delivered by a Mrs. W. A. Noble who was sent out with her husband, Dr. Noble, by the First Methodist Church in Wilkes-Barre, Pennsylvania. She had a very clear and resonant speaking voice which gave her remarks outstanding significance. Once she mentioned that it was a good practice to have a special nightdress which was not so binding about the chest as the daytime dresses were, but she did not show us a sample nightdress. She enlarged upon the necessity of free breathing for good health and condemned the layer upon layer of chest and breast wrappings. Upon my return to school I made a nightdress of my own design from a worn-out daydress given to me by my mother.

Walking to school with books tied in wide kerchiefs about their waists, girls were often ridiculed by men and boys for trying to learn, but in spite of sneers some of the girls continued for four years until graduation. One other girl and I comprised the first graduating class. We both gave orations. My topic was "Suffering Is the Seed for Joy," using the thought "They that sow in tears shall reap in joy" (Psalm 126:5). Even at the tender age of twelve I had learned the meaning of the words which I had read so often in the Good Book.

Now that I had graduated from the girls' school, Mother was again in a quandary as to what to do next. Higher education meant money. The distance to the nearest high school was too great for a child of twelve to travel alone.

Yun Sim-Sung, a classmate who was a few years older than I, had previously gone to Seoul to enter Ewha High School—the first school for girls to be established in the history of Korea—but had stayed only a couple of months because the school authorities found she was too young. When she returned home she discovered that in her absence a girls' school, Samsung, had been established in her home town. She and I made up the first graduating class of Samsung. As we talked together one day I asked Yun Sim-Sung what she was going to do after graduation and learned that she was planning to return to Ewha High School. With a flicker of hope I inquired, "How does one get into that school?"

With great assurance Sim-Sung replied, "If you have money enough for transportation, just come along with me. We can walk to Pyongyang [a distance of about 40 miles] and take a train from there to Seoul [166 miles]. If you have three won [equivalent of $1.50] for travel it will be enough."

Eagerly I sought out my mother and breathlessly told her the wonderful news. After thinking about it a bit Mother gave her consent in this manner, "If you want to go I am ready to do what I can to help. But what about tuition, room and board?"

I told Mother that Sim-Sung had said just to come along. Mother surmised that the matter was not so simple but I confidently reassured her, "Sim-Sung told me that Ewha is a mission school, and if you really want to study there will be a way."

Encouraged by my enthusiasm Mother concluded the matter by saying, "I still have the fifteen dollars given me by the Pahk family. Because I believe in tithing I will give you a tenth of that money for transportation. It will be producing for God, because you want so much to get a higher education."

And so it was decided that I should go to Seoul with Sim-Sung.

4

Life in Ewha

It was September 11, the day of my departure. Mother made up a parcel of my clothing, including a light-weight blue quilt and a pillow, and placing the tithe money in my hand she said, "You are my son; be brave. Remember the name I have given you. I never have trouble with difficulty but difficulty has trouble with me. Have faith in God and yourself and do your part; then things will work out."

My new adventure began early in the morning by setting out on foot in company with Sim-Sung and her father, who carried our bundles on his back. We walked all the way to the railroad station at Pyongyang where we spent the final night in an inn. My ticket to Seoul cost sixty cents because I was young enough to travel half fare, leaving ninety cents for educational purposes. At 1:37 P.M. on Friday, September 13, the South Manchurian express coming from Antung picked us up, along with others who were also going to Seoul.

After the newness of traveling by train wore off, I thought of the tedious treks on foot which my father had made to Seoul to attempt the National Examinations and I wondered what he would think of his little September Monkey traveling by train to get a higher education. Had he known, he would probably have given me a name like "flying dragon," "shooting star" or "roaring lion" instead of "virtuous woman."

It was raining hard when the train stopped at Kaesong, previously the capital of Korea. How interesting it was to note the difference in dialect and headdress of the women who got on the train here. Their hair was twisted into a coil at the nape of the neck and pinned whereas the women of my area wore their hair braided and wrapped around their heads. This town was famous for growing ginseng roots which were used for medicine. The people called it "magic medicine," boiling the roots and drinking the decoction. It was said to make the old feel young, the cold feel warm, and the troubled carefree.

As the train approached Seoul it was getting darker and rainier and I could not help but think of Mother and feel a little apprehensive about the future, as no notice as to my coming had been given to the school authorities. When the train arrived it was about seven o'clock and I saw electric lights for the first time, and more houses than I could count. There were wide streets with jinrickshas running back and forth. Here at last I was seeing the great capital city, center of learning and culture, site of the king's palaces and the homes of the nobles. Through this great gate flowed every variety of enterprise, diplomats, missionaries, tourists, students and merchants.

Getting into a ricksha for the first time, with my bundle on my lap and with a cover on the ricksha to keep off the driving rain, I rode with a man pulling me, sometimes through lighted streets and sometimes through alleys and between rows of poplar trees, finally arriving at the gate of a huge two-story red brick building which housed the Ewha High School. "Ewha" means "pear blossom," the name given to the school by the last king of Korea, who approved of the school.

Yun Sim-Sung and two other girls who had joined us were returning to a well-known spot. Asking me to watch the baggage on the veranda they went inside. In spite of feeling miserably alone and strange, I looked about curiously and spied a great stone building under the poplar trees, and lighted by electric lights. Later I learned it was Duksoo Palace, one of the official residences of the old king who gave Ewha its name. Curiosity has often eased me through a difficult situation; I consider it one of God's greatest gifts to His yearning, learning children. In a short time Sim-Sung came out and led me, baggage and all, to the large two-story building which housed dormitories and classrooms. In those years there were very few two-story structures and I was delighted by my first experience of climbing stairs in an interior. There was a long corridor with rooms on either side and we two girls were temporarily assigned to room No. 3. The rooms had stone and mud floors covered with oil paper, an electric light in the center of the ceiling, and furniture consisting of a chest of drawers, a low desk, a broom, dust pan, polishing cloth and pail. Making our own beds on the floor, we lay down to rest and as we were reviewing the experiences of the day the lights suddenly went out. I was greatly puzzled but Sim-Sung explained that they had been turned off from the principal's room. My curiosity soared again and I determined to learn more about electric lights. Very tired and so very lonely for my mother, I wanted to cry into my pillow but remembered Mother's saying, "You are my son; be brave!" Feeling that she was watching me I did my best to settle down to sleep in this strange place, repeating over and over, "Be brave! Be brave!"

The next morning my real introduction to a new life began. There were a few supplies, rice bowl, wash basin, soap and other incidentals which must be purchased, but my first duty was to go with Sim-Sung to be interviewed by the principal, Lulu E. Frey. When I was ushered into her office Sim-Sung introduced me as a former classmate with whom she had graduated and whom she had asked to come with her for a high school education. Miss Frey was a tall blonde, with blue eyes, a clear melodious voice, a good-looking yet determined face. In perfect Korean she asked me, "Do you have money to pay?"

"Yes, I have nearly two won [ninety cents]. My mother gave me three won which was the tithe of all she had. I spent a little over one won for railroad fare and this is what I have left."

Turning to Sim-Sung, Miss Frey said, "Are you going to help her with her room and board?"

Hesitatingly, Sim-Sung replied, "No, I could not do that."

"Then how could you bring her here without my consent?" With no answer from Sim-Sung, Miss Frey turned again to me saying, "Do you have anybody who will pay for you?" When I said I had no one who could pay, Miss Frey chided me, asking how old I was. Upon learning that I was almost twelve, she became impatient, and cried, "Child, if you are almost twelve, you must have better sense than this. You must know that you cannot get an education with two won. I don't know who you are or who sent you. You have no sponsor, except what Sim-Sung tells me. You will have to go home."

"But I can't go home. It was because I had little money that I came to Ewha. And if I were willing to go home I would not have come in the first place. Here is the only place where I can get an education."

Again Miss Frey insisted, "But you must go home. Dr. Rosetta Hall is going to Pyongyang day after tomorrow and you may travel with her." Dr. Hall, I learned later, was a Methodist medical missionary who founded a blind and deaf school, introduced the Braille system, and was responsible for the establishment of the Women's Medical College in Seoul.

Feeling this was a very crucial moment in my life, I told Miss Frey how my mother had succeeded in getting me into schools thus far and I insisted that I must stay here. After three days of pointless arguing, Miss Frey capitulated to the strong-willed child, saying that never in her life had she met such a stubborn girl but that she would let me stay on and see what she could do.

There were about forty-five resident students and most of the girls lived in the dormitory. In the dining room eight girls were assigned to each table, with an upperclassman at the head. Each girl brought her own rice bowl, spoon and pair of chopsticks. We sat on the floor around the low table and after the blessing, voiced by a teacher, one of the girls at the table would serve, each taking her turn for a week. Well-cooked rice with red beans, soup, pickles, and other vegetable dishes, salted or fresh fish were served each day, with meat on Fridays. Korean beef is very delicious as the cattle are fed cooked straw and soybeans in winter, and green grass and soybeans in summer.

There were no classes on Saturdays so we spent the day in washing, ironing and sewing. This latter chore was no simple one. In the winter we wore padded blouses made from ten to twelve pieces of cotton or silk for the outer part and seven pieces for the lining. When a blouse became soiled we had to rip it apart, remove the cotton, wash the cloth, redye it if necessary, starch it, partially dry it, then fold the pieces and lay them on a polished granite slab and beat them rhythmically with two smooth, round sticks until a peculiar luster came to the cloth. Then we sewed all the pieces together, put the cotton back, and pressed the garment with an open charcoal iron. However, the teachers soon taught us to give up the old beating method and simply iron with a flat iron. We gladly followed their advice. On Saturday we also cleaned our own rooms and each week one set of girls was responsible for the appearance of the classrooms, the chapel, halls and stairways. Baths, hair-washing and lesson preparation were also part of Saturday's activities.

Sunday we set apart as a holy day, stopping the ordinary schedule and attending Sunday School sessions followed by a morning church service. At noon, on return from church, a bun filled with sweetened bean pulp was served to us in our rooms instead of Sunday dinner. Some of the girls sold their share to others in order to get spending money. In the afternoon we read, took naps, wrote letters or chatted quietly. A Sunday supper of regular Korean dishes was served in the dining room, and we finished our day by attending evening service in the church.

Our school curriculum included English, Bible study, Chinese classics, mathematics, elementary science, physiology, hygiene, gymnasium, chorus singing and debating. I soon mastered the English alphabet, but found the sounds for *f, v, z* and *th* most difficult to produce, as such sounds are not in the Korean phonetic alphabet. Over and over I practiced these sounds aloud until I was able to enunciate them correctly. I must have sounded like a mad bee or a happy teakettle going down the halls buzzing, *"z-z-z-z-s-s-s-s"* followed by a buzzing attempt at *"th-th-th."*

Part singing was new to us as Korean folksongs were melodies only. We learned Stephen Foster songs, such as "Old Black Joe" and "My Old Kentucky Home," singing Korean words and making such beautiful harmony that shivers went up my spine. From the beginning I could never get enough music. Later in my college years we formed the first women's quartette in Korea, my part being the alto. Because halftones had hitherto been unknown to us we practiced in all our spare time, never realizing what our musical ardor must have done to the nervous systems of our American teachers.

In gymnasium class, in addition to a wide range of exercises including the use of Indian clubs we learned various kinds of ball games, such as basketball, indoor baseball, volley ball, and later tennis. More important, we learned teamwork, a new concept to Orientals in spite of our emphasis on group rather than individual welfare. Sportsmanship was emphasized, and we learned to lose a game without losing face.

Public speaking and debating gave us training in expressing ourselves and thinking questions through. This was also something new to Oriental womanhood in my country. Topics included such propositions as "Is It Necessary for Women to Have Higher Education?" and "Which Is More Important, Physical Power or Spiritual Power?" We were also trained in parliamentary procedure and the conduct of meetings. These extracurricular activities supplemented classroom work and developed the personalities of these girls who for generations had been traditionally silent and meek individuals. Self-expression and participation in group activities opened a whole new democratic way of life in thinking, working and living.

At the end of October we had our "pickling vacation" of about a week. In Korea pickles are a favorite dish. They are made of onions, garlic, carrots, cabbage, turnips, celery, hot peppers, ginger, chestnuts and salted fish in various combinations, the ingredients placed in earthen jars, then buried in the earth in a storeroom and well protected with rice husks to prevent freezing. The "pickle vacation" gave the girls an opportunity to help make the winter's supply for the school under the direction of their teachers. In late spring fresh vegetable pickles were made also by groups of girls in turn. These spring pickles were known as "temporary pickles," while the fall pickles were referred to as "permanent pickles."

Christmas, with its message of joy and peace, was our gayest season. On Christmas Eve Miss Frey invited the girls to her apartment in small groups. Under a fir tree decorated with colored balls, small candles, pictures of angels and shepherds, and dotted with bits of white cotton, were beautifully wrapped gifts, one for each girl, donated by various Methodist churches of America. My first package contained a cake of Ivory soap, a face towel, a used Christmas card with a manger scene on it, and a long flannel nightgown with blue stripes. It was the first real nightgown I had ever had and how I wished I might be able to thank the one who sent it to me. One tangerine, a bag of peanuts and taffy were also given to each of us. Then after singing Christmas carols, the favorite of which seemed to be "Joy to the World," we played games. In one of the games which made a great impression, the girls were equally divided into two lines with a teacher at the head of the line. A sentence was whispered to the first girl who whispered it to the next girl and so on to the end girl who said the sentence aloud as it came to her. When the girls heard how ridiculous this whispered message would come forth, Miss Frey would say, "Always remember how this story was distorted by repetition. Never tell anything you have heard unless you are sure it is correct. This story which you are hearing tonight about the Christ Child *is* true, and you may repeat it with assurance."

Before the end of the school year there was a festival on May

31, an annual affair celebrating the founding of Ewha, which included a May queen, the winding of the Maypole, entertainment and refreshments. Thus did a tradition of old England implant itself in new Korea.

Toward the end of my first year in high school a terrific flood occurred in South Korea. One of the teachers told us about the refugees who had little to eat or wear. Trying to think of the ways in which we might help with little of our own in the way of extra clothes or money, we decided that we would give up the good meat which we had on Fridays and send the cost of this meat to those people who did not have rice. When our decision was presented to Miss Frey she was thrilled that her girls had caught the message of love to this extent. The missionary teachers, too, decided to do without meat, and the principal was so touched by our willing sacrifice that she told us that although she would send the money to these needy refugees, she would also give us meat every alternate Friday and pay for it herself. Probably she knew we needed that meat in our diet, beside the fact that she was a warmhearted person. At that time we were not even aware how much more we learned from what our teachers were than from what they taught. Although the mission boards have consistently sent Korea a high type of teacher from the point of academic training, the big thing about the missionaries has been the fact that they have trained hearts along with their disciplined minds. The combination has made a deep impression on Korean young people in a period of transition.

One day during my high school years a missionary to India came to Ewha to visit. She wore an Indian sari and told us of the life of the Indian girls, including the untouchables. Her message so stirred us that we gathered together after the presentation and decided to give a scholarship to a needy Indian girl.

But how? Then someone suggested a thank offering. Using an earthen mitebox each girl would drop in a coin or two for the various blessings which she enjoyed from time to time. At a designated date these miteboxes were collected during a little ceremony and the contents sent to India by Miss Frey. Years later upon the occasion of my visit to the Methodist Mission High School in Lucknow, I spoke to the student body and met two girls who were supported by the scholarships sent by my alma mater. They gave me a beautiful sari as an expression of their gratitude. Upon my return to Korea I conveyed their thanks to the girls at Ewha.

During that entire first year at Ewha, my mother worked very hard to help pay my school expenses. She succeeded in earning one-third of the necessary amount and John Z. Moore, a missionary who was head of the Pyongyang district, paid the other two-thirds. It was he who had baptized Mother and me during the time I was studying in Samsung. One day near the end of the school year Miss Frey called me to her office and happily announced that she had secured a scholarship for me. Overcome with joy and gratitude, my eyes brimmed with tears as she explained further that a blind man in Wilmington, Illinois, in the United States of America, C. G. Steinhart, with his sister and her husband, Mr. and Mrs. W. H. Whitmore, had sent thirty-five dollars to cover my first year's expenses. They had promised the same amount for the next two years of high school and for four years of college, totaling two hundred and forty-five dollars. She showed me a picture of my benefactor who had become blind at nineteen but had learned Braille, determined not to be defeated by a handicap which he felt he could overcome by the power of God. Since the money had arrived for the year just closing, Miss Frey insisted on refunding to my mother what she had paid, and Mother, unwilling to use it for herself, gave it to her nephew toward his education.

With financial assistance assured by this scholarship I was able to finish high school and go on to Ewha College, which had been established during my high school days.

5

College and Prison Life

Lulu E. Frey made a tremendous impression on my life. She had been born in Ohio in the mid-1800's and was educated in Bellefontaine public schools, Ohio Wesleyan University and Moody Bible Institute, Chicago. The Cincinnati branch of the Women's Foreign Missionary Society of the Methodist Episcopal Church sent her to Korea. The idea of establishing a college for Korean women was hers. She had vision, strong convictions, and the verve for executing a definite plan. There were, of course, innumerable antipathies and prejudices to overcome in the Koreans, among them indifference, severe and biting criticism, and in many instances positive opposition. Yet Miss Frey ignored them all and in 1909 quietly started the first college class in the Ewha High School building with only three girls, Dorothy Yi, Alice Kim and Marcella Syn. Ewha College thus became the first women's college in Korea founded by the Methodist Board of Foreign Missions. This college was destined to serve as a lighthouse in the life of the Korean people, shining in the dark and tempestuous days which lay ahead.

I was in the third class of this new college, along with two other girls. But one, Pak Chang-Soon, left in her junior year while Grace Ahn died in her senior year. Having lost my two college classmates, I was left to graduate by myself. The fourth and fifth classes also produced only one graduate each, Julia Syn and Helen Kim. (Julia's husband is Bishop Hyungki Lew of the Korean Methodist Church, and in the 1930's Helen Kim was made president of her alma mater. At present Ewha Woman's University has nearly two thousand students under her splendid leadership.)

It was a pathetic picture back in the days when the classrooms contained only one scholar and the teacher, the two facing each other for days, weeks, and sometimes for the entire semester. A student really had to know her lessons and a teacher really had to use patience. One of those teachers, I recall, taught me that "a winner never quits and a quitter never wins." The addition of college classes to Ewha required a larger teaching staff. Jeanette Walter came to teach physical education; Olive F. Pye, science; Grace Harmon, music; Jeanette Hulbert, mathematics. In my junior year Alice R. Appenzeller, the first white child born in Korea to the Methodist pioneering missionaries, returned to Ewha after she had completed her education in the States, to teach English and history. Although it was Miss Frey's faith and prayers which laid the foundation for Ewha College, it was Miss Appenzeller, later the second president, who built the magnificent stone buildings on a lovely site near Chosen Christian College, a men's college, in Seoul. When Miss Appenzeller died in 1950 the whole city mourned her; the president and many national dignitaries attended her funeral. Her influence had reached all across our country. But in my student days we had very meager equipment. We also had nothing but English textbooks which made the teaching situation difficult. May I say that I was the first Ewha student to study trigonometry?

Through the medium of a college education we young women were nurtured spiritually and intellectually. Our minds were stretched! Possibly no Korean women before us had ever had such a stretching. We were interested in everything which concerned our country but also we followed with avid attention the disturbances and progress in the rest of the world.

Japan's annexation of Korea on August 29, 1910, was indeed horrifying news to us at Ewha. We felt that it was certainly the most shocking day of Korea's history. All along Japan had been promising us independence but instead had established a protectorate over Korea. Some persons in the Western world felt Japan should be restrained, that the action was unjustified and politically immoral. Most Westerners, however, did not think of the matter at all. The West and the East were very far apart in those days. Neither hemisphere had any idea that both would someday be drawn together in blood and heartache. Finally Japan annexed my country. It seemed as if the sun had set on Korea; twilight had descended; our people were groping blindly in the dark.

The impact of the annexation was beyond description. When the Japanese flag was raised in important places, several patriots committed suicide. The Japanese language had to be taught in Ewha for it was made compulsory at all schools. The internal and external rights of the Korean Government were turned over to the Japanese military government which began to exploit the people of their land and its natural resources, and deprive them of their civil liberties, such as freedom of speech, freedom of press, freedom of organization and freedom of religion. All Korean organizations, including the army, were dissolved. Men and women caught violating Japan's orders were imprisoned and often executed.

In 1911, the year after Korea was annexed, there was a nation-wide revolution in China, led by Dr. Sun Yat-Sen, ending the Manchu dynasty. In 1912 China became a Republic with Yuan Shih-kai as its first president. That same year, on April 15, we heard of the sinking of the White Star liner *Titanic*. We were terrified because Miss Frey, who was on sabbatical leave, was supposed to have sailed on the *Titanic,* but in a few days a cable came telling that her sailing date had been changed because when she arrived in England via the trans-Siberian railway her trunk had not yet reached the embarkation point.

In August, 1914, Japan declared war on Germany and captured Tsingtao, China's great northeastern seaport which Germany had leased from China back in 1898. Japan also seized Germany's Pacific islands, the Marshalls, the Carolines, the Marianas and the Palaus. Later in the Treaty of Versailles Japan obtained a mandate over all these islands. In contrast the Russian Army collapsed and the Russian Revolution was under way. In Korea we watched these moves with fascinated interest. For us the most significant news was President Wilson's Fourteen Points and we responded ardently to the policy of self-determination for small nations.

We Koreans were firmly resolved not to let Japan take root in Korean soil too long. We knew that once she became strongly established it would be very difficult to uproot her. One day news reached me, carefully and quietly told, that an independence movement was afoot, a movement engineered by the Korean common people against the Japanese military government. Acting in line with the old proverb, "No baby gets its milk unless it cries," we decided to make our cry for independence heard.

Korea was ready for such an independence movement for

our old king had died about the time the Peace Conference was taking place in Paris in January, 1919. Earlier he had been forced to abdicate in favor of his weak son because he refused to consent to a Japanese protectorate. A rumor that his death had been caused by traitors who poisoned him had aroused the ire of the people. The whole national setting was like a pile of wood soaked in kerosene; if someone struck a match it would immediately burst into flame.

On March 1, 1919, on the occasion of the king's burial, while multitudes of people packed the city to witness the funeral procession and to pay homage to the ill-fated ruler, thirty-three prominent men gathered at the Taewha Kwan, and signed the Declaration of Independence. One copy was given to a young man to be read to the throng in Seoul and another copy was sent to the Japanese governor general, informing him where this group could be found. The minute the messenger finished reading the Declaration of Independence at Pagoda Park in Seoul, the great crowd with one accord proudly raised their hands and flags and shouted, *"Mansei! Mansei!"* meaning "Ten Thousand Years!" Long live the Independence of Korea! Thus the nonviolent demonstration against Japanese rule started. It was the first genuine *people's movement* in Korean history.

The Japanese police, utterly unaware that this movement was brewing, were stunned. Actually at first they did not realize what the commotion was all about and seeing the enthusiasm of the crowd they raised their hands and shouted with the rest. But as soon as they got their bearings they struck back violently. The thirty-three were arrested along with other prominent men, women, teachers, students and even boys and girls. There were not enough jails or enough standing room in the jails to accommodate the demonstrators. In spite of Japanese torture and persecution, for over a year the shouting voices of the people kept on ringing in the villages, valleys, towns, cities and mountainsides—everywhere in Korea. But the shouts were drowned in blood and eventually the patriots were forced underground. During the Independence Movement seven thousand Koreans were killed and two hundred thousand arrested.

At the outbreak of the Independence Movement I was a teacher in Ewha College and High School, having stayed on after graduation to teach mathematics, gymnastics and music, the latter including chorus singing. I, too, had joined the great Independence Movement and had been thrilled to my very soul by the waving flags and the cries of the people. On March 10, 1919, while I was teaching a class in geometry, word was brought that the principal wished to see me in her office. There I found two policemen, one Korean and one Japanese, waiting to take me to the police station. They began to tie me up with a rope, but Miss Frey, who was determined to accompany me, told them, "You do not need to tie her. She will not run away." Explaining that this was a regulation, they proceeded to tie the rope around my waist under my coat, and holding the other end they led me to the police station. When we arrived at the gate they stopped Miss Frey, telling her that she might go no further, and in spite of her frantic claim that they could not take me away from her they forced her to turn back. As we parted she whispered to me in English, "Trust in the Lord."

Upon entering the detention station I faced a group of horrible-looking men seated before a square of cages, into one of which I was thrust. As I stepped into the cage I saw a girl whom I knew coming back from the examination room, bleeding from the torture that had been inflicted upon her. When my turn came all ribbons, hairpins and other articles with which

I might hurt myself or commit suicide were removed from my person before I was conducted to the examination room. With a background of all sorts of torture implements, including thick ropes, bamboo sticks, rubber hoses and jars of water, I was allowed to sit on a bench while I was interrogated by an examiner who had three rough-looking men standing by. The examiner began by saying, "Since you are responsible for all your students who joined in the demonstration for independence, you should be punished. Have you any explanation?"

I replied, "Although I am their teacher I cannot prevent them from taking part in what is right, and I do not feel that I am responsible for their conduct."

At this point I looked up and saw one of the burly guards with his hand upraised holding a stick ready to strike me, and remembering Miss Frey's words I silently prayed to God to help me. The hand holding the stick dropped, not a further word was uttered, and I was led back to the cage.

The next morning after sitting on the floor of the cage all night, I saw my friend again led out and led back, bruised and bleeding, and I wondered when my turn would come. That night about midnight all my possessions were returned to me and I was led outside to an old Ford automobile and was told to get in. How happy I was as I imagined I was being released and returned to my school-work. To my great dismay I was driven to a huge iron gate which I realized was the entrance to West Gate Prison. The gate swung open and I was led through a building to yet another gate, where two women guards took me to an office furnished with a table and chair for the chief guard who sat there and watched as the two women undressed me garment by garment and searched me for concealed weapons. Angry beyond expression, and resisting this indignity I cried to God again in my extremity, and when they reached my underwear they stopped, pinned a strip of cloth with the number 2221 on me and led me to cell No. 6 in solitary confinement. As the thick wooden door was banged shut and the heavy bolt drawn, I shuddered as I felt that I was sealed in a tomb.

The cell was about six by six feet, nine feet high, with one sliding window next to the ceiling, double-barred with bars and heavy screen. A four-candle-power electric light hung in the corner of the ceiling between my cell and the next one. A toilet box which sat in one corner, an empty wooden bucket with a dipper, and a filthy blue quilt infested with bedbugs and lice were the sole furnishings. There was no bed of any kind. The heavy wooden door had three openings: one, a peephole the size of one's eye at about eye level from the floor, another about a foot square in the middle of the door, and a shuttered ventilator in the lower part of the door. The cold March winds whistled, the filthy quilt was an impossible bed, and so I sat up all night as the guards passed to and fro. Not long after I had been placed in this cell I heard other steps and the bang of a door, and knew that someone had been placed in the neighboring cell, No. 5.

The next morning at five-thirty the guards came and in loud voices cried, "Get up! Get up!" One policeman and one woman guard walked down the corridor opening the peepholes and checking the number of inmates, forcing us to sit on our knees facing the door with the warning that breaking this rule would cause us to be beaten. Not knowing when the guards would sneak up quietly and jerk open my door to see if I were obedient and on my knees, I stayed in that position until my legs were swollen and black from impaired circulation. About a cupful of water was thrust through the trap door but no soap or towel was provided. Then breakfast came, distributed by women convicts dressed in clay-colored uniforms. The food consisted of a small handful of a mixture of boiled soybeans, millet and a few grains of rice which was gritty with sand, and a salty watery soup with a few bits of vegetable floating in it. Lunch was the same except for added salt. Dinner too was the same, with a tiny bit of salted fish or turnip added. Water was so scarce that there was never enough to drink and in summer the prisoners agonized with thirst. Although there was a call arrangement in the door by which a stick might be pushed into a hole in the door when a prisoner wanted something, the guards answered such summons by shrieking, "What do you want?" As a penalty for disturbing the guard no water was ever supplied when such a request was made.

Five-thirty brought the afternoon roll call. This time the guards opened the door to make the check and with the door open sounds of sighing, groaning and crying could be heard all around. These sounds greatly distressed me, and being a party to this distress, despair and tragedy myself, I resolved that should I survive this ordeal I would never cause anyone to suffer.

Every other day the toilet boxes were taken out and emptied and brought back smelling just as vile as before. Once a week a woman guard took me to the prison bath, which was a typical Japanese arrangement of a huge metal tub warmed by a fire underneath. The water was filthy, having been used by many preceding bathers, but the guard forced me to get into the tub anyway in spite of my objection. Although some of the women prisoners wore blue prison uniforms, those who were able to furnish their own clothing were allowed to do so. I took advantage of this privilege, and a friend in Ewha, Kathryn Kim, kept my clothing washed and ironed, and also supplied me with a clean quilt and pillow to use for a bed.

One day, wanting very much to have some word concerning my mother, I decided to try to send a message in my package of soiled clothing. As I hunted about my cell for something with which to write, I found a broken needle in a crack in the floor and pricking my left-hand index finger I wrote on a piece of clothing with my blood, "How is my mother?" Thereafter every time my clean clothing was returned I sought diligently for a hidden message but never found any word.

Books were banned, and days spent sitting on the knees with nothing to do were long and monotonous. Getting up when called at five-thirty each morning and not being allowed to go to bed until nine-thirty at night, I learned that the most difficult thing in life is to wait. And so long days passed by with only one hope—to be called by the court.

Hungry, lonely and worried, I prayed constantly for two weeks that somehow God would provide me with two things —something to eat and a Bible to read. In the meantime I had found a bit of companionship. Hearing a stealthy coughing on the other side of my barred window near the ceiling, I climbed on top of the toilet box to see, and heard a girl's voice whisper, "Listen carefully. I am Maria Kim; who are you?" Recognizing a friend she unfolded a plan of communication which included a series of knocks on the wall;

one knock meant "How are you?"; two knocks "Good news"; three knocks "Get up on the toilet box and talk." After this neither of us felt quite so lonely and thus the days passed.

One rainy day three knocks came from Maria's side and I climbed up to talk. Suddenly from the peephole in the door came a gruff voice saying, "What are you doing?" At the same time Maria was caught. The guards immediately took us for punishment and we were placed in distant cells without food and water for a whole day. While there a man and a woman guard came to tell me that I had broken a rule but since I had been so good otherwise they would not punish me further at that time. After the solitary penalty was over I was shifted to cell No. 7, so that an empty chamber separated Maria and me.

About noon the very next day, in spite of my having broken a rule, God saw fit to answer my many prayers. The trap door of my cell opened and a bowl of delicious well-cooked rice with broiled beef, beansprouts and kimchi (Korean pickles) were thrust through, followed by a Bible written in English. Thrilled by this direct answer to prayer, I laughed and wept as I grabbed the rice and began to eat. After the meal I opened the Bible at random, and the first words that met my eyes were, "And God said, 'Let there be light,' and there was light." "O dear God, how did you know I needed these things?"—forgetting that I had been asking Him so desperately for them in my extremity.

Twice each day from that time on the same high quality food was handed through the door and later I learned that it had been sent by Miss Frey. The Bible had been sent by B. W. Billings. Now I simply reveled in the reading of God's Word and studied the illustrative maps of the

Bible lands. Sometimes I read eight to fourteen hours a day as I followed Paul and the other early Christian characters on their journeys. Stirred by what I read I wanted God to use me just as He used Paul, and kneeling in that lonely cell I dedicated myself to His service. In those days I had plenty of time for prayer and meditation and it was brought to my realization that my people could not fight Japanese militarism by force (which they did not have) but that by prayer and Christian perseverance much could be accomplished with God's help. Certainly my people needed Christianity and the encouragement of Christian faith. Day and night I communed with God and studied His Holy Word, reading the entire Bible through once. Some verses such as "Yea, though I walk through the valley of the shadow of death, I will fear no evil, for thou art with me . . ."; "I am the vine, ye are the branches" held such special significance for me that they were veritable meat and drink. I learned much scripture in English.

One day a woman guard opened my cell and led me to an office where a Canadian missionary was waiting to see me. He was Frank W. Schofield, bacteriologist at Severance Hospital in Seoul and one of Korea's real friends. Looking me over carefully he asked, "Are you treated well here?"

In reply I simply smiled.

Then a policeman said triumphantly, "You see? Just look at her—her looks prove that she is well treated."

The visitor continued, "Do you have any books to read?"

"I have a Bible."

The policeman again interjected, "You see? We supply everything she needs."

I was led back to my cell. A week later I was called out

again. This time an American gentleman was waiting to interview me. And several times after this I was exhibited as a specimen of their good treatment because the good food and the Bible provided by my dear friends had given me a peace of mind and a happy, radiant look. (Years later I learned that the American gentleman was William L. Stidger. On my second trip to America I met him in Boston and we talked of the Independence Movement of 1919. In the course of our conversation West Gate Prison was mentioned. Suddenly he said, "Aren't you the girl who was brought to me there as proof of their good treatment of prisoners?" Seventeen years had elapsed since that meeting in the Japanese jail in Korea but this time I met him in a friend's lovely home in America.) Pleased with the impression I made on those who came to inspect the prison the guards began to take me, with head and face covered by a prisoner's hat, to the courtyard every day for fifteen minutes of sunshine and fresh air.

It must have been about a month later when my door suddenly opened and I looked up to see my beloved friend, the principal, standing there with a guard. Not a word was permitted to be spoken but each of us paled as we gazed into each other's eyes. Somehow we both felt that spoken words were unnecessary. Then the door was banged shut and I wept bitterly. That was the last time this great missionary leader and I ever saw each other for not long after, Miss Frey returned to America, and two years later died of cancer on March 18, 1921, at Milton, Massachusetts, at the age of fifty-two. She was buried in Bellefontaine, Ohio. She will go down in Korea's history.

Soon after Miss Frey's visit I was led on a rope from jail,

placed in a cart and taken to the court, which was about a mile distant, and there put in a tiny prisoner's box to await a hearing. On the way to the box I saw a young man being tortured by twisting his fingers. In my extreme resentment to this torture I silently cried to God, "God give him strength to endure, and at the same time use us in your own way to right these wrongs." In the midst of his agony the young man looked at me, and from his expression I knew that he pitied me as I pitied him, and that if possible he would have done anything he could to help me. Again the unspoken word took on a great significance. Many, many times since, I wondered what finally became of him.

All day I stood in my cage, waiting for the trial, hot, thirsty and uncomfortable. About 4:30 P.M. my time had come, and taking off my prisoner's hat a policeman led me to the judge. He said, "I've heard that you are a model prisoner and that you have behaved very well. You are a political prisoner, but remember that you can never get independence by fighting for it. You must be obedient. Be a good wife, and mother, and don't teach young Korean girls such wild ideas. You have stayed in jail long enough to understand that. If you will promise to do as I have told you, I'll see that you are released."

I spoke no word. I was returned to the West Gate Prison in a car and under guard.

By this time my old cell, No. 6, had a new occupant, the only daughter of one of the signers of the Korean Declaration of Independence. One night this young girl's voice—yelling, scolding and singing—awakened me. Her poor mind had snapped under the strain of solitary confinement and prison routine. For two weeks she did not eat or sleep, and all efforts to subdue her, including beating, failed. Finally she was taken away.

Another time, while waiting in court, I saw a former student, Yu Kwan-Soon, who also was awaiting trial. Just sixteen years of age, she had left Ewha after the independence demonstrations started and gone to her own village in South Korea. Here she stirred up her people and those of surrounding villages, making flags and organizing demonstrations on market day. She did not mind walking miles over desolate mountain roads to carry her message for independence. Her father, her mother and brother, along with many others, were shot by the Japanese for taking part in these demonstrations, and eventually she had been arrested. Subjected to great torture and sentenced to seven years of imprisonment, she had appealed to a higher court and was sent to West Gate Prison. My heart was moved to do something for this young girl, but I was quite helpless. Still I felt great remorse for her plight. One night I heard her cry, "The Japanese have killed my mother, my father, my brother and village people and taken away everything," and when she persisted in leading her cellmates in a demonstration the guards took her out and beat her. Months later she was flogged to death.

There were eight girls in the neighboring cell, No. 8. As I sat alone one night about nine o'clock, I felt something drop in my lap. It was a tightly folded note. Thinking that I might be dreaming, or even losing my mind, I hesitatingly opened it and read, "We are with you. We will all soon be released, so don't worry." The note had been forced through the tiny opening where the electric fixture was fastened to the ceiling. The girls had accomplished this feat by piling their quilts in the corner and climbing upon the pile. They had risked punishment in order to cheer and comfort me since they were afraid that I too might lose my mind.

On July 24 I was once more taken to the court. Facing the same Japanese judge who had questioned me before, he said, "It is the court's decision to release you under fifteen dollar bond. Since your friend, Dr. B. W. Billings, has posted your bond, you may go."

Thus my freedom was secured. When I got into the black carriage which would return me to the jail, there were Esther Whang, Maria Kim and Julia Syn, whom I knew, and also a woman in a blue prison uniform. When we got out at West Gate we four girls were told that we would be released, but the woman was told that she was to die. The poor condemned soul did not understand what they said because they spoke in Japanese. Again a huge wave of pity swept over me for the plight of this ignorant, yet motherly woman.

We girls were taken to a room where our belongings were returned to us and instructed in the things we should and should not do after we were released, since we were to be on parole. The warden addressed me, saying, "You were the happiest person we ever had in this jail. Will you tell me the secret of your joy?"

"It was my religion!" I told him.

Exactly at 11:00 A.M. on July 24, 1919, the horrible iron gate of the West Gate Prison swung open wide enough for a person to pass through. Japanese guards were standing on both sides of the gate with bayonets fixed. We four girls were let out of that iron gate. Freedom at last! To me, or to anyone else, certainly freedom—physical, mental and spiritual—is one's most precious possession. That was why my people had started the Independence Movement.

When we stepped out of the iron gate, we were met by Dr. and Mrs. Billings who had been waiting there since 8:30 A.M. They were the Methodist missionaries living next door to Ewha. I used to visit with them and play with their children, Paul and Helen, and often read books with them. As a matter of fact, Dr. and Mrs. Billings and I read Shakespeare's *Merchant of Venice* together and after we had finished reading it they gave me the English name of Portia because I, too, had once been disguised as a boy. It was Dr. and Mrs. Billings who had persuaded the judge to allow me to have a Bible while I was in jail. From the jail they took us back to Ewha. Marie E. Church, who took Miss Frey's place during the summer months, welcomed us. We were to remain in her care for the month of our parole. I shall ever be grateful for her genuine affection for all of us.

After arriving in Ewha, my first impulse was to go home to see Mother but I was required to wait out my parole. However, I soon learned how she had been getting along. She had found it necessary to pull dried stems and roots of grain for fuel. Nevertheless her faith had not faltered. She persisted in her struggle against circumstances and made her own way in order that she would not be a burden to anyone. When her brother had brought the news of my imprisonment by the Japanese, she had prayed, "Dear God, there is no one to do anything for my little girl except her missionary friends. Bless them in your service." This was the burden of her prayer every morning and evening as she turned her face toward my prison in Seoul, 180 miles away. As she gathered her roots and stems, wrapped them in a cloth, carried them home on her head, made her fire and cooked her rice, she thought of me, hungry, distraught and bereft, and when she placed the cooked rice in her mouth it tasted like sand. As stories of the maltreatment of Korean girls reached her ears she wondered why she, an old woman, was allowed to live. Actually she, too, had suffered unmerciful beatings across the legs because she had taken part in independence demonstrations.

Word also came of the death of Mrs. Lansa Ha not long after my arrest. Her daughter, Jaok, was a chum of mine and to me a romantic figure because her mother was the first Korean woman to be graduated from an American college. As a child she had been trained as a dancing girl in Pyongyang. To become a dancing girl one had to be pretty, intelligent and attractive. These girls often came from poor families but many also came from better-class families that had lost their economic position and needed the money obtained by furnishing a likely dancing girl. These girls were encouraged to develop personalities along with learning to dance, sing, play an instrument, smoke, drink and entertain men. They had to be able to converse with men on almost any topic from history and politics to philosophy and art. They were the professional artists and entertainers for the public since wives and daughters were not allowed to do such things. During our struggle for independence some of these girls were ardent patriots. One true story from the past concerns a Jinju dancing girl who was required to entertain a famous Japanese general on a beautiful summer evening. They were occupying a lovely pavilion built on the bank of a wooded ravine overlooking the river. The girl maneuvered her admirer into a position on the open porch so that while he was embracing her, she was able to throw herself and him down the embankment to perish with him in the river below.

Mrs. Ha had become the concubine of a wealthy man but she had a passion to educate herself further so that she could serve her country usefully. Although she had a girl child of eight months—my friend Jaok—Mrs. Ha convinced her so-called husband that she should have an Occidental education. She went to America, finished college with a B.A. degree and returned to Seoul where she taught at Ewha. When Jaok died of tuberculosis Mrs. Ha asked me to stay with her for a week. After that I visited her often and was proud of her political influence. Later she was sent by our country on an important mission to the Paris Peace Conference but died en route while in Peking.

Another bit of information was that the Treaty of Versailles had been signed in June. Behind my back the whole map of Europe, the Near East, Africa, Asia and the Pacific islands had been changed. It was as if a terrific earthquake had shaken the very foundations of the earth, effecting new boundaries and alignments. Definitely, for the first time in history, the people had begun to get hold of political power. Ever so many countries, both great and small, had been made into republics all at once. For the coming seven years of my life, I lived in that aftermath of World War I and Korea's Independence Movement. It was a period of privation, dissension and internal disorder in all the countries where the form of government had been changed. My own personal life at this time reflected the disorder and privation.

6

In the Belly of the Whale

Two weeks after my parole ended, one of my pupils, Kim Young-Sook, brought an invitation to dinner from her fourth brother. The invitation included Julia Syn, who had been released from prison with me. Kim Young-Sook was one of my favorite pupils, tall and slender, with black wavy hair, a fair complexion, dimples and sparkling eyes. She stood out in my favor not only because of her extraordinary beauty and charm but also because of her scholarship and modest, shy manner. Without hesitation we accepted the invitation. It was the first time we had been invited out to dinner since our release.

The next day, an hour before dinnertime, Julia and I walked to Young-Sook's brother's home, about a quarter of a mile from Ewha. It was an early September day, clear, and refreshingly cool. After having stayed for so long in that hot and humid jail, this experience seemed too good to be true.

When we arrived at the house Young-Sook came to the gate to welcome us, followed by a tall, good-looking young man whom she introduced as her brother, Kim Woon-Ho. I was struck with his likeness to his sister. He, too, had black wavy hair. Also he had broad muscular shoulders.

Later I learned he was an athlete and football champion. He wore Korean white which indicated that he was in mourning for his father who had died two years previously.

The tile-roofed house was well built. We were led into the inner court for ladies where Young-Sook's mother and two sisters, one older and one younger, greeted us most cordially. Taking off our shoes we entered the living room and were seated on lovely red and blue brocaded silk cushions around a large low black table inlaid with mother-of-pearl, depicting the scenery of the Diamond Mountains. On the walls hung two scrolls, one a painting of a beautiful but fierce tiger standing on a high rock and the other a painting of green bamboo. On either side of the living room there were two bedrooms furnished with typical Korean brass-bound chests in one room and mother-of-pearl inlaid chests in the other.

Dinner was served on that beautiful low table. Young-Sook brought in tray after tray of well-known Korean dishes tastefully prepared—beef, pork, chicken, fish, and several vegetable dishes with kimchi, soup and white rice. For dessert they served fresh apples and dried persimmons. At the table Young-Sook's mother, brother, Julia and I ate and talked while Young-Sook and her sisters waited on us. The dinner conversation was constrained because of the tense feeling regarding the Independence Movement but what Woon-Ho said seemed to be well-chosen, timely and safe and I was very much pleased with his tact and courtesy. His mother was very much like my mother in character and temperament except that she was nine years younger than my mother. By the time we were ready to leave the Kim home, I felt completely at ease. Since it was night, Woon-Ho offered to accompany us back to school, a daring procedure in those days. The half-moon was hanging low in the sky as Julia and I walked with him in the breezy night. None of us talked much. Modern though we claimed to be, we were shy. Before we parted at the gate of Ewha, Woon-Ho and I gazed at each other thoughtfully there in the soft moonlight. That night was the first time in my twenty-two years of life that my emotions were stirred by a young man. Of course I had met many men at church gatherings but none had touched my heart.

Up to this time I had not thought much about marriage, because my missionary teachers were the models for my life. Most of them had remained single, consecrated and devoted to their mission in life. I had always said that I would not marry just for the sake of being married for I loathed the Confucian scheme of using girls primarily as instruments for continuing the family. My theory of a perfect marriage was something like a chemical formula—H_2O = water. When a young man and young woman have something to contribute to each other theirs should be a perfect union. But if a couple were united because of an infatuation the marriage would never work. That September night, after meeting Woon-Ho, I tried to analyze my feelings but now I realize that I was too close to new emotions to evaluate them sensibly.

The next day, Young-Sook brought me a note from her brother, and I sent him one in return. From that time on we corresponded, Young-Sook acting as carrier of the letters.

In the meantime the Japanese again imprisoned me for one month during December of that year, this time for membership in the Korean Women's Patriotic Society. After my release my friendship with Woon-Ho progressed and he confided to me the fact of a previous marriage. He said he had been married when he was twelve years old to a girl one year older. At that time his father was a merchant living in the west side of Seoul and quite well-to-do. Woon-Ho was the fourth son in a family of four brothers and four sisters. His father, who was an old man, had wanted to see him married and consequently he had married while still a child. After the wedding ceremony he and his bride returned to their respective homes, seeing each other only on holidays. He continued his schooling at Paechae Boys' School, a brother school to Ewha, and his wife did not come to live with him and his family until he was sixteen. Then the final marriage ceremony took place but when they came together there was such a personality clash that on their first two wedding nights they stayed up all night instead of going to bed. What could he do? Legally married to this girl he must follow family tradition and the wishes of his family, even though he was unhappy with the girl. One year later, after his father had died, he became the head of his own family—himself and wife in this case—and he began divorce proceedings.

In Korea divorce is permitted, but not frequently taken advantage of. It would have been very easy and entirely acceptable to society for him to have taken a concubine, but he was a Christian and the Christian Church did not sanction concubinage. Under Japanese civil law, a divorce could be easily consummated if both parties agreed to it, but traditional Korean law required the consent of the bride's father if he were living, or if he were dead an older brother or uncle or the male responsible for the girl's marriage should give consent to the divorce. On the male side consent must be given by the father, if living, otherwise the man concerned usually made his own decision. If ever a girl needs male relatives it is at such a time as this.

The young bride's relatives gave their consent to Woon-Ho's divorce and it was so decreed, with alimony for the divorced wife.

All this had transpired some time before Kim Woon-Ho had met me. Now he was free to marry the girl of his choice and he asked me to be his wife. And then began a struggle for me. Although it was legally right to marry this man whom I loved, the Church was greatly opposed to marriage to a divorced person and almost if not completely ostracized members who so married. My heart was torn between loyalty to the man I loved and loyalty to the Church and the God whom I also loved and served. The Church said "No" and my heart said "Yes." As usual, I prayed for God's guidance, constantly entreating Him to show me the way.

And truly God began to make His way plain. Alice R. Appenzeller had succeeded Miss Frey as principal of Ewha. One day she called me into her office and said, "We want to send you to the General Conference of Methodist Churches in America. You pray about the opportunity and we'll work for it." Not long afterward the First Methodist Church in Seoul voted to send me to the meeting of all the churches in the district where the representatives would be chosen. Here they learned that I was too young to be a delegate. However, the determined Miss Appenzeller said, "We will send you to America anyway, as a student!"

A month went by and nothing further happened. Then I was again called to Miss Appenzeller's office where I was told that I had been granted a full scholarship including tuition, room and board at Ohio Wesleyan University in Delaware, Ohio, and three hundred dollars in gold was ready for my passage by steamer. This greathearted woman urged me to apply immediately for a passport. Was this God's answer to my prayers for guidance? I was in love, but here was a wonderful opportunity to get a further education in America, the dearest dream of every Ewha girl. I knew it would be difficult to get a passport which must be granted by the government of Japan. Having been a political prisoner I knew that if I got a passport it would be only by God's power. So I prayed, "God, if I get a passport I'll know it's your will for me to go and if I don't get a passport I'll marry." The time of decision was approaching. It was either a higher education or marriage. In the meantime letters went back and forth between Woon-Ho and me every day.

One day in June soon after school closed the passport arrived! Stunned by the miraculous occurrence of the seemingly impossible, I knew I must go. When I broke the news to Kim Woon-Ho, he wrote: "I congratulate you on your good fortune. As for marriage, there is a certain ideal age. Why not marry now and go together to America later to study?"

Now I was in a worse quandary. God had made the passport possible but love called so strongly that even in spite of my pledge to Him I wavered. Going to America after our marriage was an entirely new thought. Remembering the old Korean proverb, "The life of your daughter and the course of a stream depend on what you do to guide them," I knew that I was making a decision which would determine the course of my life. Torn between emotions and intelligence, I struggled for two weeks in an agony of confusion until at last, in spite of the wonderful ways in which God seemed to have shown His will, I decided to be married.

Miss Appenzeller was heartbroken with disappointment when I returned my passport and told her of my decision.

Weeping, and begging me to reconsider, she said, "Induk, you are very unwise; you don't know what you are doing. This emotion will pass. Go to America and study for a couple of years and then if you still want to marry this man on your return, how beautiful your marriage will be."

However, no amount of argument or persuasion availed. I had made my decision. My friends also advised me not to marry this man, and my mother, who had sacrificed so much to educate me, did everything within her power to induce me to reconsider. When I actually told Mother that I had decided to marry Woon-Ho, she said, "You have almost built a mountain and now you are going to tear it down." She reminded me that we had always been desirous of helping others find the new way of life which we had found in the church and school, and that we must always set the right example in all things. She tried to make me see that this man would not make a proper husband for me; for one thing, he was only a high school graduate while I was college trained, and while a difference in education did not always make difficulty in a marriage still it was an important consideration. Finally, and most important of all, Mother had heard that Woon-ho had a concubine and she was positive that I could never change him into the kind of man I would have him be. Disbelieving this final charge and feeling sure that any difference in background would be no handicap, I insisted that I would marry him, in spite of Mother's disapproval. With a final reminder that "all that glitters is not gold," Mother gave up the struggle and committed me to God.

Most of the Ewha girls and their teachers went home for the summer vacation. As I packed all of my possessions ready to leave the school permanently, my heart was filled with misgivings as to the wisdom of my choice, and through the terrific conflict within my heart I knew I was being disloyal to God and also to myself. After I had finished packing I lay down to rest while waiting for the ricksha to come to take me to the station, and suddenly I heard an inner voice saying, "Induk, be a missionary." I protested, saying, "But I can be a missionary even if I am married." So when the ricksha arrived it carried me to the station and I went back home to Mother for my wedding.

In the meantime Mother had been hoping and praying that I would change my mind, and so when I arrived home and told her that I had come to be married, she turned her back on me and said, "Why did you come home? Why didn't you stay in the city where your husband-to-be lives?"

I was at home about a week and the news spread through the little village of Dukdong that I was planning to marry a divorced man. The claim was made that I was marrying him for his money. There was now a great wall of misunderstanding between Mother and me. It was sad that we two who had shared hardships and made sacrifices and suffered together for the sake of my education and the Christian way of life, now found ourselves so estranged! Since Mother absolutely refused to have anything to do with the wedding, I finally returned to Seoul for the nuptials. Mother was very bitter and as we parted she said, "Never come back to me since you have refused to listen to me," and so I left extremely downhearted.

At four o'clock on July 7 a very quiet wedding took place at the home of the groom with only a few close friends present. Without Mother and my most intimate friends, the occasion seemed more like a funeral. The wedding reception was held at a restaurant during a rain that came down in torrents. Was the rain an indication of the stormy years which lay ahead of us? The heavy rains had so flooded the towns along the Han

River that for several days we were unable to travel, but when the waters finally subsided we went on our honeymoon, and returned to live in my husband's household.

For a fortnight we were very happy. Then I had a rude awakening. One day I heard my mother-in-law and her three daughters talking about my husband. I could scarcely believe my ears when I heard his mother say admiringly, "He had far more will power than I ever dreamed. Who would have thought that he would give up his concubine when he married?" I learned later that she was the prettiest dancing girl in Seoul at that time.

Shocked that I had been so deceived during our ten-month courtship, I could hardly believe what I had heard. It must be a mistake; I must have misunderstood. Then one of his sisters added, "He can be very strong-minded when he wants to be."

So my mother and friends had been right after all. Anxiously awaiting Woon-Ho's return, bitterly disappointed in him whom I had trusted, and angry with myself for being thus betrayed, I struggled hard to regain my composure. When he came in I said quietly, "So, you had a concubine and sent her away when we were ready to be married! That is true, isn't it?"

If he had confessed there could have been some foundation for forgiveness, but he shouted, "It's a lie!"

Thoroughly angry, now that he had added a lie to the wrong he had already done, I replied, "Who is telling the untruth, you or your mother?"

He did not answer my questions or deny further but instead boasted, "Don't you know a man's privileges? You should have been a man too!"

In a flash I knew now why my mother and father had wanted me to be a boy. I also remembered that I had made the choice which had brought me to this humiliation. Recalling the story of Jonah, which I had read so many times in my Bible, I cried to God, "Truly God, I am in the belly of the whale. You called me to go on your errand and I refused. Now I am paying for my disloyalty to you." What could I do? I was married to this man, and it appeared that all I could do was to make the best of it.

Months passed. My husband had no earning power and no training. He had made a settlement both with his first wife and his former concubine, thus spending his entire inheritance. He was deeply in debt. The house where we expected to live when we were married had burned to the ground just after we had furnished it and shortly before we actually took possession, so that we lost all our belongings. A silver vase which I had loaned to a friend was the only article which was not lost, and it was returned to me after the fire. Clasping it in my hands I realized that what I had kept to myself I had lost and that which I had shared with others was saved. As Christ had said, "He that findeth his life shall lose it: and he that loseth his life for my sake shall find it." Right there I determined to share what I had with others.

Finally we rented a tile-roofed house outside the East Gate near a Buddhist temple. We had to go into debt to buy furnishings and to pay the rent so that we were unable to meet our expenses and soon moved again to smaller quarters. This house was near the city sewage outlet and therefore much cheaper but still it was more than we could afford. The next move was into a thatch-roofed cottage near the slaughter house. The open sewage stream, the stench of slaughter and the agonized screams of the cattle were almost unbearable. Finally there was not even money for rice and Woon-Ho's mother, who was being supported by her oldest son, shared with us some of the rice from her own allowance. Each time we moved my husband's creditors followed him, and since he did not own any property they could only attach our furniture and threaten to take everything if we did not pay.

Money was so scarce that even sending a letter was difficult. Once when I wanted to mail a letter to my mother and had only two of the three sen necessary, I asked my husband for another sen and he shouted, "You know I do not have it!" I told myself he was totally unable to understand me, my needs, my talents and my pride. Perhaps he was, but it was my pride which suffered most acutely.

One night, in deep anxiety, I tried to talk with him about what we must do, as we could not go on in this manner. When I suggested that he must find work not only to pay our debts but to keep alive, he became so violently angry that he punched and kicked me. Crawling into bed like a beaten animal, I suffered even more greatly from disillusionment and disappointment than from the blows. Unable to sleep, I got up in the middle of the night and in desperation walked to Namsan (South Mountain) which was one and a half miles away. Facing a dead end emotionally, I was lost in darkness and my faith was so shattered that I decided to commit suicide. My mother still held resentment toward my conduct, my friends were aloof, my husband disloyal, a lazy man, a liar and a brute. There was nothing left to live for. I finally chose a branch on which to hang myself. Pondering all these things had slowed down my physical reactions.

All of a sudden I came to myself! A great light dawned in my mind and soul. Aloud I said, "What a fool I am! To think that I would take my own life!" Falling upon my knees I asked

God to forgive me. Remembering the Bible scene of Jacob wrestling with the angel, I felt that I was really holding onto God as I communed with Him further. I could not ask additional aid of Him but I determined to do my very best insofar as I had strength, and let Him do the rest.

I walked back home and found the gate locked. Answering my knock my husband angrily inquired where I had been. Instead of answering his question I said with a newborn air of authority and determination, "Talk sense. From this time on I am going to map my own future. If you wish to come along with me, that's up to you." He realized that I was intensely serious.

My attempt to get a teaching position met with no success. Opposition was strong. My friends were unable to help me because of the feeling against me. The winter was long and cold, and many times I was both cold and hungry. My husband failed to co-operate in hunting work but instead he stayed in bed until nearly noon and then when he did get up he demanded a meal. He would not even build the fire which sometimes took me ten to fifteen minutes to get going before I could cook a handful of rice.

Our first baby was born in the spring, a perfect little girl. We named her Iris. As I held her I knew moments of deep joy. It seemed as if my joy could not rise to the surface and yet I knew it was there. In a strange way she seemed to justify my mistake in marrying, or rather to offer herself as an undeserved blessing. I loved her a great deal.

However, the advent of our first born made no difference in my husband's attitude. Thinking that further education might make him more capable of supporting us, one of his brothers and I sent him to Japan to study. The baby and I then moved in with his mother, adding two members to the already large family, which consisted of the maternal grandmother who was seventy-seven years old, the mother, two unmarried daughters, and the second son and his wife. Untrained to cook and sew as typical Korean girls do, I did not know quite how to fit into this family. How thankful I was that my mother-in-law was sympathetic, wise and understanding, so that when my turn came to cook she took my place even though it made the others very jealous. The oldest son with his wife and children lived near by, and he also had a concubine. The other son with his family lived about a block away and gossip flowed back and forth like a muddy stream. To make matters worse Woon-Ho's sisters compared me with his first wife who had been divorced from him. Life was often very difficult and I realized that to stop this gossip I must either do the household tasks much better than they or I must work and make money.

On the day that Iris was one hundred days old a friend came to call, and when she saw the environment in which I had to live her heart was moved. She told me that Queen Yun's sister and sister-in-law were looking for an English teacher and that if I were interested in the position she would intercede for me. The lessons were to be given once a week for one hour, and the pay would be twenty-five dollars in gold a month. She urged me to try and when I talked the matter over with my mother-in-law she was pleased and consented to the plan, offering to keep the baby for me at lesson times.

The position was obtained, and in June I returned to my teaching career. The minute my earning power was apparent the hostile atmosphere of the household changed, and the gossiping in-laws became friendly. Seeing this transformation I realized that in order to experience freedom and independence in a genuine way, Korean women must achieve earning power. It was about that time that my husband returned from Japan, penniless, and no better educated than before.

But in the fall of 1921 the Women's Bible School asked me to instruct in music three mornings a week. When the liberal-minded missionary principal, Anna B. Chaffin, came to call on me to ask if I would teach the choir, the family opened their eyes in admiration and the atmosphere showed a further tendency to clear.

The school had a three-term system with the school year beginning in April. At the beginning of the second semester, in September, 1922, I was asked to teach music and English every afternoon at Paewha Girls' High School founded by the Southern Methodists. The following summer I was invited to teach music at another institute in the evenings for five days a week. So I had a full schedule. I worked literally sixteen hours daily, Monday through Friday, and skipped lunch because of poor transportation facilities and distances between places of duty. On Saturdays I had one class at the home of a Miss Yun.

Upon returning home in the late afternoon, I would often find my brother-in-law napping under a mosquito net in the coolest place in the living room and my husband taking his nap in the breeziest spot in our quarters. Both men were being waited on hand and foot by the womenfolk who brought basins of water, soap and towels for washing, and salt for them to clean their teeth when they rose in the morning. After their ablutions were cared for, they were brought food on trays. Thereafter the remainder of the day was spent visiting friends and playing chess or checkers. The only persons in the household who worked were my mother-in-law who cared for baby Iris, the old cook who prepared the food and was a recent addition to our establishment, and I, who earned the money.

Two years passed, during which enough money was saved to buy a thatch-roofed house just back of Paewha Girls' High School, and then baby, husband, old cook and I moved into it. The house was tottering and old, really almost ready to be torn down. But I was grateful and happy to have a home of my own, although I knew I would miss my mother-in-law.

The first thing I did after getting settled in our house was to invite Mother for a visit. She had never really been reconciled to my marriage for her wounds were too deep, but nevertheless she wanted to see her first grandchild. She decided to come with her brother, the one who had formerly persecuted us so much. However, some time previous my uncle had given up smoking and drinking and had become an ardent Christian. Mother had prayed for him for fifteen years and was deeply happy when he was converted.

And so on one August day just before school began Mother and Uncle arrived at South Gate Station. As I was escorting them home Mother said, "You know, you yourself cut the top off the tree. Your teachers and friends were watching you, expecting you to make good but you cut short your own growth. The only way now to make the tree look well again is to wait until the branches grow up to cover the cut top. That is a long, hard test, but never give up. The mistakes you have made can be turned into fertilizer to make the tree grow."

When Mother took the baby in her arms for the first time, how delighted she was with her granddaughter. She was also pleased with the lovely name I had chosen for her, the name being a combination of the character for wisdom and the character for the iris flower, one of the five queenly flowers beloved by artists. The Korean iris has a delicate fragrance which permeates the entire court where it blooms. Later, I overheard my mother talking to the baby. She said, "Remember, you must live up to your name. And remember also, you are a third-generation Christian!"

When Iris was two years and five months old, another baby girl was born. All of the family wanted a boy and I tried not to be disappointed. Using the same character for wisdom and the character for another queenly flower, I named her Lotus. I chose this flower because although it grows in the mud, a lowly place, an exquisite flower develops. And we hoped that this baby too would thrive under her lovely name.

When Lotus was a little over two years old, it suddenly dawned on me that my family might keep on increasing. I already had on my hands a dependent and irresponsible husband. How could I rear and educate more than two children? After much thought I called on the principal of the Women's Bible School, Mrs. Chaffin, and requested her help in obtaining a scholarship in America. She tried to discourage me, reminding me that two children were a great handicap. Going home on a streetcar that cold February evening in 1926 I was almost discouraged when I unexpectedly met Rubie Lee from Statesboro, Georgia, a missionary who was teaching music with me at Paewha. When Miss Lee asked me why I was traveling so late, I told her my story and ended by saying, "I haven't given up hope yet. I know I have difficulties but I love to work out problems. I strive hardest against odds. If I could only get a scholarship!"

"Wait a minute!" Rubie exclaimed. "I have a sister Nellie in Wesleyan College in Macon, Georgia. I'll write to her and see what she can do."

Breathless with the prospect, I cried, "Do it; and I'll pray

God to open the way for me again!" I felt I would now recognize His leading, whatever it might be, and I knew that this time I would follow it.

It took one month for a letter to reach America, and I waited eagerly for a reply. One day about a month later Miss Lee met me when I arrived at school. She said, "I have a cable saying 'COME—LETTER FOLLOWS. DR. QUILLIAN.' "

Thrilled with what I knew was a direct answer to prayer, I now faced another difficult task in getting my husband's consent. One day when he was in a particularly good mood, I talked with him quietly and logically. "For our future, for Korea as well, it would be a wonderful thing. I can speak English and you can speak Japanese. If I go to America to study for a couple of years and you go again to Japan to study, we will both be perfecting our knowledge. Later if the way opens up and God is willing, you may come to America too." Pointing out the future possibilities I told him that I had everything ready, the scholarship, money to take care of Iris and Lotus, and even money for him to study in Japan. Then and there God performed another miracle for my husband said, "That would be fine!"

When I gave my mother the news that I was going to America her face shone with joy and she said, "I am very happy, for this is the answer to my prayers. Your decision to go to America is about the wisest one you have made since your marriage. In my judgment you made a grave mistake in your marriage. Since then every time you tried to make a move forward, you were pulled backward by your husband because he is just a typical Korean man exercising power over his wife. I am glad you have made up your mind to jump, and if you are going to jump I hope you will jump high and far."

"I am going to jump a long way," I replied, "all the way across the Pacific."

My mother's benign smile warmed my heart as she nodded her head. "I knew you would, sometime, my son."

Since I was to leave my children at home, Mother and I talked long and seriously of the days past and of the years to come. She said to me in her usual philosophical way, "Life is like a river. Unless it reaches a precipice and falls it can never make a waterfall. The higher the cliff the more magnificent the display. So it is with life."

Of course leaving my children was the big problem, not so much from a practical point of view as from a tearing at my sense of identity with them. In Korea it is customary for the mother-in-law to have the final decision in most matters affecting the welfare of her son's children. Traditionally she is more responsible for them physically and morally than is their mother. Moreover, Korean grandmothers enjoy this relationship to their grandchildren and every mother looks forward to becoming a grandmother. It did not seem strange to any of the family or neighbors that I should be leaving the girls with their paternal grandmother. If my husband had taken an official position abroad or even in another part of the country I would be expected to do the same thing. Nevertheless it seemed very strange to me to think of not seeing my own babies for two whole years. Often my heart grew weak at the thought but my mind did not weaken. I set my eyes on the future. It would be better for my children, for my country, for the future of our family life—if it was to have any future—and for me as a modern woman to go after the rest of my formal education. I must go where the training could be had.

Our arrangement was that money provided by me would be

paid each month by one of the teachers at the Bible School, Hortense Tinsley, to my mother-in-law. I knew that our cook would be almost as faithful as my mother-in-law in caring for the children. My mother-in-law was one in a million, if I may use the vernacular. She understood my position and was sympathetic and unprejudiced. One day she said to me that her son and I would never be happy unless he could be made to respect my position as an intelligent modern wife. Like my mother, she realized that unfair practices had bound women to their mates. I felt very grateful to her and very safe in leaving my children with her.

Passports usually took from one to six months to acquire and were often refused but our passports came in thirteen days. To me that was a good omen. Steamer tickets had already been engaged, luggage was soon packed and we were ready to sail into the unknown.

7

Jump Across the Pacific

Early on the morning of August 2, 1926, our journey began. It was a rainy day, but many friends had come to see us off. As the ricksha gathered momentum I looked back and saw the playful Iris, five, with a pillow on her back to represent a baby, and the old cook with Lotus, aged three, on her back, and numerous other members of the family and friends waving good-by. I felt their love enveloping me like a cloud, like the cloud which led the children of Israel, and I was inexpressibly grateful to God for this second chance He had so graciously given me. Closing my eyes to hold back the tears, I prayed within my heart, "Dear God, you have been so kind. I will never again forsake you."

Soon my husband and I were on the train to Pusan where we would take the steamer to Japan. A friend, Lee Inae, who was going to America to be married, was to be my traveling companion. The trip on the fine South Manchurian train was comfortable and very interesting to me, for I had never before traveled south of Seoul. The southern women seemed much more masculine than the women of my own area. In Seoul women were occupied mainly with their household tasks, but as we approached the coastline I saw women pulling nets out of the water, piling fish into boats, curing fish, and doing all the other jobs pertaining to the fishing industry. I learned that farther south on the island of Chejudo, the women were famous for their expert diving for the fish which lived among the rocks. Wearing hemp dresses and trailing a rope on the end of which a gourd floated while they were below the surface, these women carried a kind of hooked implement with which they gathered their prey. They could stay under water for five minutes or more at a time and were so adept that they were called "Women of the Sea."

Arriving at Pusan we went directly from train to ship. The Japanese customs officers checked our credentials and quizzed us regarding our reasons for travel, all but examining our thoughts to be sure we had no subversive plans. They were unable to understand why a young mother desired to go to America to study but when my husband assured them that he had given his consent they seemed satisfied. Woon-Ho turned to me in his usual domineering manner and said, "You see, if I didn't give my consent you could not go. I have the key in my pocket."

Once more I was disturbed by the power which Korean men held over their wives who could not move one inch without masculine consent. If my husband had said a single word of disapproval before these inspectors there would have been no chance for me to go on. Brought up with the Christian concept of the sacredness of personality and the freedom of the individual, it seemed unfair that I was absolutely at my husband's mercy.

At dusk we stood on deck and watched the ship move out of the beautiful harbor with its background of mountains and twinkling lights. I was so enchanted by it all that I actually pinched myself to ascertain whether I might be dreaming. From childhood my desire to go out into the world had been something more than a strong urge. The little village of Monyangtul where I was born was located in the hills above the beach at the extreme end of the port town of Chinnampo. When I was very small I used to stand and watch the boats, both small craft and large foreign steamers, plying in and out of the harbor. Often I climbed up high into the hills back of our house to dig roots to make our vegetable dishes and couldn't help but look out over the ocean. To the north and south we were hemmed in by rugged purple-blue mountains. But to the west there was nothing but the vastness of the Yellow Sea. As I grew a bit older I learned that from Chinnampo one could sail to China and on to India, and on up to Europe, or to Japan, and on to Hawaii and so to America, or north to the Russian Maritime Provinces. The urge to travel was strong in me.

After going to bed that night, my thoughts were occupied with my two little girls. I wondered whether they were sleeping or missing me. And before I knew it I was weeping. My mother's voice resounded in my ear. . . . "If you are going to weep when you think of your girls, you had better not go." Immediately I dried my tears and prayed to God to look after them. "They are your children as much as mine. Even more than mine! I am your child, too. Keep us all in the curve of your arm. So near to you our Father, we are near to each other."

Early the next morning our ship docked at Shimonoseki. The harbor was filled with fishing boats, the mountains were much greener than the brown hills at Pusan, and the people on the whole looked shorter than the Koreans. They were very active people, tense and diligent. They talked little but when they did speak it was in a quick, low voice. Because they were free politically they were themselves, while our folks in Korea was submissive. The same independent spirit was obvious in stores, streets, trains, on farms and fishing boats.

We went directly to the Tokyo train which was much smaller than the South Manchurian train. Watching from the train window as we passed through villages surrounded by farms, I noted that the houses were neatly kept and that their thick thatched and tiled roofs sloped more steeply than Korean roofs, which are curved and often turned up at the ends like Chinese roofs. Japanese houses seemed to reflect the Japanese disposition which is quick and sharp. It was very evident that in this country no land was wasted, every inch was planted, while in Korea much land was left to make boundary lines between fields. Everywhere men, women and children seemed to have the desire to help their country become the foremost in Asia, if not in the whole world. From the train we also saw the great Fujiyama, highest mountain in Japan, standing like a sentinel over the foothills. It was apparent why the people revered Fuji. It seemed more than a mountain; a spirit given form and majesty.

Tokyo was the first metropolitan city I had ever visited and for a few days we were taken on sightseeing trips by the Korean Y.M.C.A. secretary and his wife, my college friend, Pak Seung-Ho. (She was later betrayed by her own Communist daughters, sent to jail, and eventually put to death because she would not accept communism.) We saw an exhibit of the earthquake damage of 1923 in miniature. It was truly a remarkable replica; every walk of life was portrayed as caught at the very moment of the disaster. In the three subsequent years practically all that had been destroyed was already replaced. The indefatigable industry of the Japanese is admirable. Their adaptability was also evident for the young people were already wearing American clothes. They made use of everything new that would improve their standard of living. Even with the great Pacific between Tokyo and San Francisco, the Western impact was so strong that I felt I had already reached America.

We were also impressed by the fact that no matter how poor the family, the Japanese knew how to enjoy picnics and outings together. They are great sightseers, especially of historical sights and famous views. The contemplation of beauty was almost another form of religion and in no place was love of beauty and order more apparent than in their ceremonial teas. Somehow their versatility and adaptability to Western ways seemed enhanced and strengthened by their firm loyalty to their own ways and ideals. I observed these people closely for their power was so keenly felt in my own country, and I wanted to understand their background and motives.

The time for parting with my husband was drawing near. Through a friend in Korea he had made preliminary plans to study poultry husbandry at a farm which was operated by two brothers whose student helpers received their room, board and training in return for work done. According to the agreement he was to stay for at least three months, after which he would be free to seek work elsewhere. With these arrangements completed my mind was at ease concerning his welfare.

Miss Lee and I prepared to sail on the Dollar liner *S.S. Wilson* on August 9. Again when my passport and credentials were checked my husband reminded me that if he did not give his consent I would not be allowed to make this trip. I acquiesced. But I thought to myself that God could overrule even a husband and I went ahead with all the necessary details and boarded the steamer at the appointed time.

Since there were only two classes of accommodations, first class and steerage, and since neither Miss Lee nor I had much money, we took steerage. Our tickets from Yokohama to San Francisco cost sixty dollars each. My baggage consisted of a woven reed traveling case in which I carried my Korean Bible, an English-Japanese dictionary, toilet articles and Korean clothing for each season. My husband waited on deck while a porter took our luggage and led us down stairway after stairway until it seemed to me that we would surely arrive at the bottom of the sea. Finally we reached the large room for women where there were two tiers of berths all around the walls and down the center of the room with only sufficient space to pass between them. Each berth was furnished with a blanket and pillow. I was given a lower berth and Miss Lee the one directly above me. After settling our baggage we climbed the stairs to the lower deck at the stern of the boat and waited with the other passengers and their friends and relatives who had come to bid them bon voyage until such time as the gong sounded for all visitors to go ashore. My husband left us. Independent though I was, I felt very small. The passengers lined up along the rail and their friends stood on the wharf, while colored paper streamers were thrown back and forth so that each passenger was connected with friends on the shore. Some were crying; others laughing. I smiled within my heart as I thought that this moment was a springboard upon which I would catapult into new life. My husband and I waved farewell as long as we could see each other.

Soon we were well out on the Pacific Ocean sailing eastward to the West. When we returned to our quarters we found fifteen women besides ourselves, including Chinese, Filipinos and Japanese, most of them going to Hawaii. Dinner was served at five-thirty and as there was no dining salon for steerage passengers, we lined up for rice and a stew made of meat and vegetables served from large cooking kettles presided over by stewards. We sat on the lower berths to eat, after which we returned the plates and received dessert which consisted of fruit from Japan.

No amusements of any sort were provided but this made little difference when the passengers began getting seasick. There were summer storms and when we looked through the closed portholes and saw our ship rising to the crest of a huge wave, then dropping into the trough, it was too much for us. All became seasick. Each of my steerage companions moaned and cried in her own tongue that she was going to die. I was glad I was not traveling first class and unable to enjoy its advantages! After three days I recovered somewhat and said to myself, "Well, before I die I am going to see as much as I can." So I climbed the three flights to the steerage deck and walked until I was stopped by a sign reading "NO STEERAGE PASSENGERS ALLOWED." Stunned by the realization that even here, far away from the domination of the Japanese, there were still limits beyond which I might not pass, I walked back to the rail where I rested my eyes upon the vast ocean and limitless blue sky. I was fascinated by the flying fish rising from the water, flying three or four feet, and then dropping back. Noticing my enjoyment, a deck hand told me that if I would watch carefully I might see a whale. As I looked toward the unbroken horizon I was stirred to think that this Pacific Ocean must be made up of water from the rivers of many countries. Moreover it is big enough to accommodate millions of fish, many varieties of vegetation and marine life, and to cover submerged mountains and ancient cities. Overcome by the majesty and all-encompassing power of God, I prayed that He would help me to be great and good enough to understand and care for all people as the ocean made room for all waters.

From then on I enjoyed the trip to the fullest. One of my delights was the way we moved our watches back an hour or more each day. On Sunday we had a special dinner and as we had crossed the international date line on Sunday, the following day we had Sunday dinner again. One of the women had a birthday on Sunday with a second birthday the following day. About bedtime on the ninth day we noticed that many passengers were rushing to the rails and looking off into the distance. Miss Lee and I followed the crowd. Soon we saw a lighthouse and the twinkling lights on the shores of Hawaii. Everybody began to speak excitedly in his own language, but no doubt the cry was the same—"Land, the land. We see the land!" I thought of Columbus and his sailors and recalled a poem by Joaquin Miller which I had learned in literature class at Ewha, and had translated into Korean.

> Then, pale and worn, he kept his deck,
> And peered through darkness. Ah, that night
> Of all dark nights! And then a speck—
> A light! a light! a light! a light!
> It grew, a starlit flag unfurled!
> It grew to be Time's burst of dawn.
> He gained a world; he gave that world
> Its grandest lesson: "On! sail on!"*

Our steamer arrived in port at six o'clock the next morning and most of the passengers hurried their preparations to go

* Copyright, 1909, by C. H. Miller; 1936, by Juanita Miller. Used by permission of Juanita Miller.

ashore, many of them to stay, the others to browse around as they wished until that evening at six when the boat would sail again. Being steerage passengers, my friend and I were not allowed to go ashore unless we were bonded. About eight o'clock, Mr. and Mrs. C. H. Minn, Korean friends of Miss Lee's, came to visit us and learning of our need for a bondsman, they hurriedly posted a one thousand dollar bond for each of us. How generous of them! In my mind I compared the value placed on a person in Korea and in America. In Japan while on parole my required bond was only fifteen dollars; in Hawaii I was worth one thousand dollars!

Ashore the air was cool and delightful and the solid earth felt good beneath our feet. People everywhere appeared carefree and at peace, whether they were Chinese, Japanese, Korean, Filipino or American. Here was a miniature world made up of many peoples and they seemed happy living alongside one another although they differed in many of their customs and in their dress. Having come from a country where the women had only one pattern of dress, variety being achieved in material and workmanship, it seemed strange to see many different styles worn by the women here. Weighing the matter, I decided that although Korean uniformity led to economy, it gave no opportunity for ingenuity. Here ladies had to exercise their mental faculties in order to have dresses different from others and this to me seemed an advantage.

Beautifully kept lawns spilling over with gorgeous bright-colored flowers and the absence of fences reminded me of the speaker who had come to the girls' school in Korea and had described to us the wonders of this island. I could scarcely wait to taste the fruits he had mentioned.

Soon after arriving at Mr. and Mrs. Minn's home, luncheon

was served and not having had any Korean dishes on the ship, the rice, broiled chicken, lettuce and various vegetables with soy sauce tasted like home. We ate abundantly. Then came the large mellow bananas, mangoes, oranges, pears and pineapples, even more delicious than I had imagined them. How I yearned to have some of these foods flown to my family at home!

After lunch our hosts took us for a jaunt to Waikiki Beach where we saw surfboard riding for the first time. We also visited the Korean Christian Church and Korean Institute, both founded by Syngman Rhee. I was overcome with longing when I saw Korean children playing in their school yard. All too soon it was time to board ship. Some of my former schoolmates from Ewha came to the boat to see us off, bringing armloads of fruit, and flower leis which they placed around our necks. Even the ship seemed reluctant to pull away from the shore when the band played "Aloha."

All of our bunkmates had left ship at Honolulu but when Miss Lee and I returned we found that seven strange women were to share our quarters. Since these new passengers were typical carefree young Hawaiians the entire atmosphere was greatly changed. Most of the time was devoted to dancing, singing popular songs and teaching others the songs so they could join in. One of the favorites was "Yes, Sir, That's My Baby." I amused the ladies greatly when I asked whether or not they were singing about a real baby. With a full moon and a Hawaiian guitar, this little band had much happy fellowship there on the steerage deck while the first-class passengers were being entertained by professional musicians. During our stopover in Hawaii we had learned that by paying a small fee we could have Japanese food in place of the regular ship's fare, so for the rest of the trip Miss Lee and I had trays of Japanese food for both lunch and dinner.

After several happy days we sighted San Francisco harbor early in the morning. For some time sea gulls had been following the steamer and now there were great flocks of them hovering about the ship waiting for cast-off food. Even for the gulls America was a land of plenty. A flock of American battleships also rode Golden Gate harbor, while a bevy of gasoline tanks roosted comfortably on the hills. The skyline of high buildings, the bustling harbor traffic and the busy bridges typified the enormous industry and activity of the great country toward which I had so long turned my eyes.

First-class passengers disembarked first, after which the immigration officers called the steerage passengers. When I told the officers that I had come to America as a student there was no question of my eligibility for entry, but we were courteously told that we must go to Angel Island for a physical checkup. We were taken to the immigration station in a small boat, arriving there about eleven o'clock. The entire detention station was enclosed in wire netting and after the officers and immigrants went inside the gate was locked. Reminded of my experience in the Japanese prison in Seoul, it seemed strange that I must begin my student days in America in this manner, and I was further worried lest I might not pass my physical examination and thus be barred permanently from my new life.

We were taken to a large women's dormitory where Chinese, Negroes, Mexicans, Spaniards, Italians and others were herded together. After we had settled our suitcases on the beds which we would occupy, we were taken to the dining room where Chinese chop suey and rice were served to both men and women together. In most Oriental countries men and women ate separately but this was America. Then we returned to our section and eagerly awaited the doctor who would make the examination and tests. In this interval Miss Lee and I chatted with other women and found language no barrier. We learned that some of the women had been detained here for more than a year due to red tape; others for six months, three months or a week. We wondered whether we might also have to stay for a long time while some unforeseen complication was unraveled.

After dinner there was supervised recreation for the women, including games and dancing. While Miss Lee and I sat watching the others, a Negro woman of enormous proportions came up to me and urged me to join the dancers. When I protested that I did not know how to dance, she grabbed me in her arms and jittered me around the floor until I was happily exhausted. That was my first and last dancing lesson.

Next morning we were called for our examination and our reports proved so favorable that before noon we were taken to the dock where we were surprised to find three Korean friends, Earl K. Paik, editor of one of the Korean papers of San Francisco, T. W. Kim, Miss Lee's fiance, and Mrs. J. H. Yang, their friend. Our rapid progress through detention at Angel Island had been due to their intercession.

As we rode the cable cars up and down the hills of the city I noticed men and women traveling together, happy and carefree. I was particularly impressed with the protective interest which the men showed toward their women companions as they helped them into the cars and preceded them to help them off. It seemed that it was "ladies first" in America while in Korea "gentlemen first" was the rule.

After a pleasant drive we were taken to Mrs. Yang's home where we met Mr. Yang and their three small children (all of whom later graduated from college). We ate delicious California seedless grapes, sweet and juicy watermelon and honeydews. I learned that Mr. and Mrs. Yang ran a restaurant where for ten years many Koreans coming through San Francisco had been invited to eat as their guests. I stayed with them for ten days, including two Sundays, on which days we attended the Korean Christian Church. Here I met an old Ewha friend, Mrs. Alice Hahn, which made America seem more homelike, for we had lived together in the same dormitory for several years.

Mrs. Yang, a cultured and bighearted woman, gave me lessons in etiquette and social graces, showing me how to comb my hair effectively, and explaining American customs. One afternoon she took me to a big department store and bought me shoes, stockings, underwear and a tan winter coat with a red collar. In fact, she took me over as one of her own and helped me in numerous ways to adjust myself to the American way of life.

When the time came to make the trip across country my friend advised me concerning traveling tourist style. Knowing that I woud be confused by the menus in the dining car she packed sandwiches, hard-boiled eggs and fruits in sufficient quantity to last until I reached Chicago. Then Mr. and Mrs. Paik and Mr. and Mrs. Yang took me on the ferry and settled me aboard the train. I was simply amazed with the fact that in America everything is made as easy as possible for travelers, with the train leaving directly from the ferry and the ferryboat coming right up to the wharf.

Leaving these new friends in San Francisco I felt that I was again leaving home. They stood on the station platform waving as the train pulled away. For the first time I was traveling entirely alone. I felt this parting from my American-Korean friends more keenly than when I left Pusan or Yokohama and when their waving hands and smiling faces were lost to sight I whispered to my never-failing friend, "Dear God, go with me."

I was looking out of the window when the porter came along and showed me the women's room, the water fountain with its paper cups, and explained that when I was ready to go to bed he would make up the berth. I was grateful for his kindness; he made me feel a welcome guest in his country. Then I watched the landscape speed by until darkness fell. That night I adored my traveling bedroom with its net hammock for my clothes and its tiny electric light. The clackety-clack of the wheels made me think back to my first train ride to Seoul. Now I was many years older and five thousand miles from home but still on my way to school. I offered a special thanksgiving to God, for it was marvelous how day by day and hour by hour I had been led by Him through His helpful people along the way. Then I prayed for my two little girls who were probably just getting up as I was going to bed. I prayed for everybody everywhere. My heart was brimming with gratitude and joy.

My first view the next morning was of ground covered with dry, scrubby plants six to twelve feet tall the like of which I had never seen before. My fellow travelers told me that they were sagebrush. One man went on to say, "Someday we will find a way to utilize this barren soil. If you go to Boise, Idaho, you will see how such badlands can be transformed by science." The thought that the barren soil of Korea might be made of use to the people kept my mind occupied for a long time.

As the scenery changed I was stirred with the might and beauty of the mountains and gorges; they had masculine strength and immovability. Our mountains in Korea, not so high nor so massive, have a more feminine quality. Having come from "Little Switzerland," as Korea has so often been designated, I was mountain conscious. Not to underrate our terrain, for our highest peak is eight thousand feet, I must mention our Diamond Mountain area, known far and wide as the most scenic and impressive section of our country. This mountain chain has twelve thousand peaks interspersed with ancient Buddhist temples. The Chinese have a saying, "I wish I were born in Korea to see the Diamond Mountains before I die."

Next came the rolling flatlands with their miles of green grass, not yet browned by frost. In the farmstead scenes I recognized the house and barn but my friendly seat neighbors had to explain the silos and windmills. I was surprised at the many dead trees lying on the ground; in my land every stick is made use of. The situation of farmhouse and barns and outbuildings in the middle of acres and acres of farmland was far different from my Korea where the farmhouses are all grouped together while the farms themselves lie some distance away. American farm life seemed much more convenient. The extent of land owned by a single rancher awed me completely; such scope of property ownership is almost inconceivable to us Koreans.

Traveling day and night and day and night again, I could scarcely believe that this was all one country. Some time later I heard a story of a German who had saved enough money to make a sightseeing trip to America and on arrival in New York took a transcontinental train to San Francisco. After some hours the train stopped and he inquired, "Is this San Francisco?" "No," came the answer, "this is Harrisburg." Another long ride and the train stopped again, and again he made the same inquiry and received the answer, "No, this is Pittsburgh." When the train arrived in Chicago he thought he had surely reached his destination, and when he was assured that he was only halfway to San Francisco, he shook his head and said, "I always admired Christopher Columbus for discovering America—but how could he have missed it?"

At the Union Station in Chicago I was met by a Korean friend, William P. Lee, who wanted me to see as much of Chicago as was possible in two days. My first "sight" was the depot itself. As I looked about at this huge, magnificent station with its great pillars, numerous ticket windows, information service, Western Union desk, magazine stands, lunch bars, and even a nursery, as well as numerous gates to trains and exits, I was absolutely agog. When we took a taxi I was fascinated with the tick, tick, tick of the meter as it turned over and over, adding the cost of the trip, but I was a little apprehensive as to its effect on my pocketbook. The fare was seventy-five cents and the gentleman paid. Translating the cost of this ride into the Japanese currency prevailing, I realized it was double the cost of a twenty-five-mile return trip by rail from Seoul to Inchon. In all of my years of travel since that time I have never forgotten the seemingly tremendous price of my first American taxi ride.

Our destination was the main branch of the Y.W.C.A. where my escort introduced me to the two Choy sisters, Hawaiian-Korean girls who spoke excellent English and were cordial and friendly. Mr. Lee left but called for me again that afternoon and together with the Choy sisters we took a taxi. Riding down Michigan Boulevard with the meter ticking busily, I was not quite so concerned this time about the cost. My mother would have said that was luxury's wooing way. Dinner at a restaurant was followed by a ride on the elevated trains. In contrast to the dim street lights of Korean cities the myriads of twinkling colored lights of Chicago seemed like a fairyland. The lights of Michigan Boulevard alone could have made all of shadowy Seoul bright.

The next day a visit to Marshall Field's department store was first on our list. It seemed to me strictly a Western idea to offer such varied services, including nursery care for the children of shopping mothers with bottle service thrown in! Everything from a bridal outfit to a home could be purchased here. We covered every part of the store with resulting leg ache. That night following my policy of seeing as much as possible wherever I went lest I never again have the opportunity, I visited the Planetarium where the reproduction of the sky moved me deeply. As we went out into the night, there in the real sky were the same stars we saw in Korea. The magnitude of the earth and of the other planets impressed me with the smallness of man. And yet God had endowed man with a soul. And his soul knew wonder, love, gratitude, joy, and also gusts of homesickness.

The next morning I took the Dixie Flyer. By and by the porter announced that we were crossing the Mason-Dixon line, explaining that it was an imaginary division line between the North and the South. When the Negroes were required to go into a special car I was perplexed. Why should they be second-class citizens? Then I recalled the class distinctions which prevail in our Korea where we have three classes: aristocrats; middle class, consisting of professional people and white-collar workers and landowners; and the others who must work with their hands. In those days lording it over all classes were the Japanese, our conquerors. Furthermore, our class distinctions operate to limit educational opportunities for those of the lower level. I reserved judgment, realizing that there must be a reason for this strange American custom; since I was to spend two years in Georgia I would have ample time to study the problem.

As the train sped through the country, I asked the porter why so much cotton was left on the plants and he explained that the best of the crop had been harvested and that what was left was not worth the cost of picking. I thought how many cold Koreans could be kept warm by this ungleaned cotton.

The next morning when I went into the dining car for breakfast I was placed at a table where a lady was already seated. Realizing that I was a student from a foreign country, she asked me where I was going and when I told her she was delighted because she was a teacher of English at Georgia Wesleyan. Now I had a friend! When the train arrived at Macon I was invited to share her taxi to the school. It was September 13 again, and very warm as we rode through the quiet streets of the town to the college buildings situated on a hill. As we drew up before a four-story red brick building we were greeted on the veranda by a group of student Y.W.C.A. members. I felt happy and relieved when the student president told me how eagerly they had looked forward to my coming. She took me to my room on the second floor and after freshening up I was escorted to the dining hall with its electric fans and maid service. Here I was taken to the college president's table, where Mrs. William F. Quillian, wife of the president, greeted me so warmly that I really felt welcome. As I ate dinner with this charming family, which included a son Bill and a daughter Christine and Grandmother Quillian, I could scarcely believe that my dream had come true and that I was dining with the family of the president of my college.

8

American Student Days

Registration day was September 15, 1926. I entered in the junior class and my course included Bible, philosophy, psychology, English history, English literature, sociology, physical education and music. I also added swimming. Two Chinese girls, Ling-Nyi Vee and Ada Lee, registered ahead of me. They were younger than I, pretty and charming, and they spoke good English. Chinese and Koreans have always been like cousins. I made an appointment to talk over my affairs with my college president. After thanking him for my scholarship I told him that I was willing to do anything he suggested to help earn this scholarship. In reply he said, "As long as you have that spirit you will be guided." I never forgot those words.

That evening the student Y.W.C.A. had a get-together. How wonderful it seemed that upperclassmen were appointed to help acquaint the newcomers with routines during their first few days in their new surroundings. All sorts of games were played to make us feel at home. Big red apples were served for refreshments and my "big sister," who was younger than I but an upperclassman, took an apple and after biting from it herself, handed it to me for the next bite. This gesture sealed a friendship which was to last for life.

Classes began the next day. Psychology proved difficult with its strange terminology and abstract ideas. I felt almost buried under the abundance of assignments. Chapel service came just before noon and when Dr. Quillian addressed the student body he said, "The aim of Wesleyan is to help all her students to set as their goal—God first, others second, and self last." He explained that life has four dimensions—height, depth, width and length. One's ideals constitute the height; the number of good deeds done rather than span of days constitute the length; convictions determine depth; and sympathy and understanding of others determine the width.

Mail time after lunch brought a letter from my husband and my heart sank when I saw that it had been posted in Korea. "Life at the chicken farm in Tokyo was too hard and so I came home to prepare to come to America." He then told me of our two daughters. "Iris is her grandmother's child and she seems content and does not appear to miss you much, but Lotus misses you a great deal." Then he told me that about ten days after my departure Lotus had been awakened by a cock crowing and had said to the old cook who was her nurse, "Country grandma, is that cock crowing because he wants to see his mother too?" Reading these words brought a rush of tears and a closing-up of my throat. Once again recalling Mother's words, "If you are going to weep when you think of your girls, you had better not go," I swallowed hard and said within my heart, "Someday, my little ones, I will make it up to you. I will make you very happy."

I was puzzled as to why my husband had left this opportunity in Japan to return to his former aimless life, when it dawned on me that the family education of the boys and men in Korea was at fault. Usually the oldest son was taught to assume all the responsibilities as a successor to the father, whereas the younger ones were brought up more or less free from care. Being a fourth son my husband had no doubt been a victim of this system. Further, he was very handsome and spoiled by the womenfolk of his family and fawned over by girls outside the family. He had sporting instincts, was musically inclined including a wonderful voice, but absolutely no sense of responsibility had been taught to him. I pondered what course I should pursue in the future in his behalf.

On Sunday when I went to church I was referred to a Sunday School class taught by Mrs. G. E. Rosser, who was a professor of Bible at Wesleyan and whose husband was also a Bible teacher. There were about thirty young women in the class, mostly business women, and at the close of the session I was invited to say something. As I had never made an extemporaneous speech in English I demurred, but Mrs. Rosser insisted, saying, "All long distances start with the first step. Just get up and start and if you need me, I will help you." Then I stood up and told them the story of how my mother had disguised me as a boy and sent me to a boys' school. They seemed delighted with my story. Afterward Mrs. Rosser invited me to become a member of the class and said she would expect me to say something every Sunday, suggesting that I write what I wished to tell and then memorize it. She added, "Who knows but that you may become a public speaker someday if you are willing to do your best now."

About a month later the Mulberry Methodist Church gave a party for the Wesleyan girls and the Mercer University boys. As a mixer each girl and boy was given a number and then told to find his partner who had the same number. As I went about looking for my partner a tall red-haired young man asked me what number I had. I said mine was 99. He said, "You are looking for a lost sheep. I am 99." Then we were called to the center of the floor, tiny black-haired, five-foot Induk, the September Monkey, and her tall, red-haired, six-foot partner, and everyone laughed at the combination.

Before the semester was over I was receiving invitations to speak in and around Macon. Dr. Quillian's promise that I would be guided and Mrs. Rosser's prediction concerning my becoming a speaker were beginning to be fulfilled. Churches and Sunday Schools often paid for my services. Mrs. Rosser's class also voted to give me two hundred dollars toward my education that first year.

At Christmas I had an invitation from a schoolmate, Mabel Chastain, to visit her home in Calhoun, Georgia, for the holidays. As I had experienced Christmas for several years in Ewha I felt quite at home with these new friends, but the New Year's Eve celebration was different from anything that I had ever known. The wild ringing of bells, noise-making of every kind, and the happy shouting of New Year's greetings by all astonished me, especially when I was told that similar celebrations were going on all over the country. I could not help thinking of our New Year's Day in Korea for which we make great preparations. We clean the house inside and out. We make new dresses or if we cannot buy new material we wash and freshen our old ones. We prepare special food. Most important of all we try to pay off all our debts and clear up all existing differences of opinion among our family, friends or neighbors so that we really start a *new year*. I think the Korean New Year is more practical than the American.

On New Year's Day we all drove to Lookout Mountain near Chattanooga, Tennessee, and went up the mountain on the inclined railway. Here we saw several states spread out in panorama before us with the Tennessee River winding through, and as I looked at this beautiful landscape I thought how significant it was that my first New Year's Day in America was spent in this lovely place and that my future lay before me like a landscape.

The holiday was soon over and I returned to Wesleyan and resumed classes with renewed vigor. Understanding slang and colloquial expressions was most confusing as my English was bookish and stilted. Words pronounced the same but with different meanings, such as grip meaning to clasp, an illness, and a piece of luggage, just didn't add up. Pronunciation too was very difficult. In Korea I had learned the Middle Western pronunciation as my teachers were graduates of Ohio Wesleyan and the rolling r was one of the sounds it had taken me seven years to learn. Now here in Georgia people dropped their r's and drawled. This too was not easy for my Korean tongue.

However, from the second semester on I was in the full swing of college life. Every morning a group of girls from our dormitory had morning watch in the living room before going to breakfast. Loulie Barnett, who was a professor of music, was our leader, and thus was established a happy mood and tone for the day's work. Every evening after dinner the girls would gather in the stately lounge to sing such songs as "Yes, We Have No Bananas" and "Pack Up Your Troubles in Your Old Kit Bag." Jazz and the Charleston were popular. Girls wore clothes with low waistlines and short skirts almost up to the knees, and small cloche hats.

Then some sensational news burst upon us. Lindbergh

made his non-stop solo flight across the Atlantic and became our hero. Overnight we all turned air-minded and were flying all over creation in our imaginations. The way the people welcomed Lindbergh home gave every young American—including me—an incentive to do some daring and adventurous deed. This enthusiasm, I found, is one secret of America's progress. Some of our Korean young folks were also caught up with the spirit of flying. Oppressed as they were by the Japanese, flying offered them release and a feeling of space and freedom. A young woman by the name of Pahk (no relation of mine) learned to fly in Japan but on her maiden flight to Korea her plane crashed and she was killed. Her ambition to fly was not too foreign to my own ideas at that time.

Plans were made for part of my summer vacation to be used for a six-week course at Lake Junaluska, North Carolina, where Dr. Quillian and his family had a summer home. Since one of my professors, Anne C. Wallace, was driving to Black Mountain, North Carolina, she took me with her on my first long trip by automobile. As we drove through the western part of the state with its green mountains I was impressed by the fact that here in America even the trees were allowed to grow to their very fullest and best while in Korea of necessity they are often cut for use before they are fully grown. The abundance of wild flowers and wild life filled me with joy and thanksgiving.

When summer school was over I still had several weeks of vacation left and desiring to make the most of every opportunity, I accepted an invitation from Mr. and Mrs. H. S. Yun, who had come from Korea to study at Columbia University in New York. Mr. Yun was Queen Yun's brother.

When I arrived at Pennsylvania Station I felt at home since I had been at Union Station in Chicago, but upon going outside and seeing the man-made canyons and forests of tall buildings and the endless crowds of hurrying people I was quite dazed. For one week I did nothing but roam around taking in the sights with my royal host and hostess.

There are four cities in the world that are different from all other cities: Venice, a city built on islands; Istanbul, a city built on two continents; Peking, a city of tile-roofed houses; and New York with its skyscrapers. One day, while we were riding in a taxi along the East River, the driver said, "The great city of New York is made up of five boroughs: Manhattan, with one great big stone foundation; Brooklyn, the most populated; Bronx, the poorest; Queens, the largest in area; and Richmond, the tiniest. Well, ladies and gentleman, New York has a symphony of its own, with an orchestration of six million people from all over the world. If you stand at Times Square for ten minutes it is probable that you will see representatives from practically every nation pass by. New York is the great trading center of the world and has everything. One can live here very cheaply or most luxuriously, as he pleases."

With five weeks of vacation left I decided to try to earn some money, so I consulted the want-ad columns in *The New York Times,* knowing that in America one could always find open doors if one looked for them. I found an ad wanting a woman to work afternoons five days a week in a private home. Accompanied by Mrs. Yun, I applied for the position. Mrs. Yun was also working as a housemaid in New York. In spite of her royal rank she was one of the most democratic women I ever knew. My prospective employer was a young woman living in an apartment on Riverside Drive; she was looking for a maid to clean her apartment and prepare dinner. I was engaged to begin the following Friday. When I reported for duty I did the cleaning work assigned but my employer went out for dinner. On Monday she advised me that I should get a better position, preferably one in a doctor's office where with my education and good English I could take telephone messages, and do other more professional duties. Evidently I wasn't much of a cook!

With four weeks of vacation still left I went to Macy's department store where they wanted an Oriental girl to work five days a week selling almond cakes at a counter conducted by a Korean. I secured this job and learned to sell as well as to pack goods for shipment, receiving fifteen dollars a week. This experience gave me a new perspective on the American public, besides training in package wrapping which in later years proved of great value. I have no doubt wrapped hundreds of relief packages for my kinfolk and refugee friends in Korea. I worked at Macy's for three weeks, and the forty-five dollars which I earned gave me a start for the fall semester.

Now I was a senior with all the special privileges that rank entailed. Contests between classes were held in playwriting and staging, and I was chosen to play the wife of Columbus in a production of that title. Our play received the prize. It was my first experience in acting and I thought of my monkey sign under which I was born.

That year the opera *La Traviata* was presented in Atlanta with Mme. Galli-Curci in the leading role and I was given a ticket by Mrs. Quillian. The beautiful costumes, the expert staging and the birdlike voice of Mme. Galli-Curci were a never-to-be-forgotten experience. Later I also had the privilege of hearing Paderewski and Mme. Schumann-Heink.

The Quadrennial Convention of the Student Volunteer Movement for Foreign Missions was to be held in Detroit, Michigan, from December 28, 1927, to January 1, 1928. Once every four years interdenominational students and professors who were interested in foreign missions came from all the states and Canada to attend this conference, and Mrs. Quillian suggested that it would be a wonderful opportunity for me to attend also. Recalling the old proverb, "God helps them who help themselves," I wrote to the secretary of the Korean Student Association in New York, Harry Whang, asking whether there was any provision for helping students attend this convention. By return mail I received the reply that they would send me twenty-five dollars if I could take care of the balance of the expense which was estimated at a total of seventy-five dollars for travel, room and board. When I told Mrs. Quillian she said that the student Y.W.C.A. had already voted twenty-five dollars toward the expenses involved, and so with fifty dollars of the necessary amount assured I decided to make the trip with the confidence that the other twenty-five dollars would be provided when needed. Six of us, chaperoned by Eleanor Neill, professor of religious education, made the trip. When we got off the train in Detroit we were chilled to the bone by the bitter cold but it reminded me of home and we all hoped that it would snow before the conference was over.

The sessions of the convention were held in the new seven-million-dollar Masonic Temple and ours was the first group to make use of this fine building. There were three thousand college students of all denominations from the United States and Canada with overseas students, including several Koreans, from thirty countries. Led by John R. Mott and others, we heard many stirring addresses.

On New Year's Eve the hoped-for snow arrived to the special delight of the Southern students who had never before seen snow. We played in it, making snowballs, snowmen and forts. Some stayed up all night as the city welcomed the New Year with bells and shouted greetings. When I returned to my room at about 1:00 A.M. I found a telegram from the general secretary of the Student Volunteer Movement, Jesse R. Wilson: "WE WANT YOU TO SPEAK TOMOROW MORNING FOR FIFTEEN MINUTES FROM TEN FORTY-FIVE TO ELEVEN O'CLOCK TO THE ENTIRE CONVENTION ON THE TOPIC 'WHAT JESUS CHRIST HAS MEANT TO ME.'" I almost wept for joy that this great opportunity had come to me to speak to these thousands of young people on the subject nearest my heart. With only nine hours to prepare my talk I was grateful for the training I had received in the churches.

At the appointed hour I went to the office back of the auditorium where I met the two others who were to speak on the same topic—a converted Mohammedan from the Near East and a Negro from Africa. After I was introduced I began by saying "Happy New Year" in Korean. Then I told them that according to my thinking, of all the discoveries made in the latter part of the nineteenth century, the discovery of womanhood in Korea, as representative of all Asia, was the greatest of all. This discovery was due to Christianity by means of which my mother had been privileged to embark on a new way of life and through her I in turn benefited. I told them of my experience as a student in the boys' school in Korea and testified to God's wonderful presence with me during my five and a half months in the Japanese prison. Although I used only eleven of my allotted fifteen minutes I was stopped several times by their applause and I had to take a bow to silence them. Actually, I felt humble.

The convention closed that evening and as we were preparing to leave it dawned on me that I still needed twenty-five dollars for my return trip. While I was trying to make arrangements to borrow the sum, a letter from the Student Volunteer Movement was delivered to me, expressing thanks for my message and enclosing twenty-five dollars!

Back at school I worked harder than ever. At the beginning of the last semester Dr. Quillian called me to his office saying that a gentleman from New York wished to see me. I was introduced to Weyman C. Huckabee, from the main Student Volunteer office, who asked me whether I would be available as a traveling secretary for this organization for the year 1928-29. He said that so many requests had come from colleges for me to speak, as a result of the delegates returning from the conference in Detroit, that they would like to employ me at a salary of seventy-five dollars a month plus all expenses.

As this offer had come to me unsolicited I believed it was a God-given opportunity but I did not accept it immediately for I had to decide the larger problem whether to return to Korea as soon as I received my degree or stay on a while with the hope of doing graduate work. On the American side of the question—or was that really the Korean side?—I felt that I would probably never get back to the States and that whatever education I ever hoped to have must be had while I was in the place where the education *was.* Moreover, my worth to my country and to my Church was greater if I had the authority of additional training. Third, and not without influence in the back of my mind, I am sure, was the fact that I liked to learn. But on the other hand, my husband and children were in Korea.

It was Woon-Ho who was my continuing problem. Looking back, I realize that no doubt I was also a problem to him. He had married himself a wife who would not accept her traditional place, who would not countenance his having a concubine or any other extramarital relations; a wife whom he could not punish through lack of material comforts because she got out and earned her own living; a wife whose standards all down the line were not compatible with his. He had long since given up the idea of coming to America. Neither the studying nor the physical work which he would have to take on, such as waiting on tables or any of the things which American college students do to earn their way, were congenial to him. Never a frequent letter writer, he had finally ceased to write. Letters from friends, reporting on the condition of my children, had also ceased to mention him. I knew things were not going well with him but I also knew that neither he nor the children were in financial need for I always managed to send money home.

In my heart I could build up quite a case for the children's needing me but with my mind I knew they were well cared for indeed, and that if I returned they would probably continue to live with their paternal grandmother, as I would myself, for we would have to have a home which suited my husband. Finally I decided to postpone my return and accept the call to work with the Student Volunteer Movement.

In June I received my B.A. degree after which I went to Teachers College at Columbia University to have a summer school of work toward my master's degree. During the first week in September a council meeting of the Student Volunteer Movement was held in Kalamazoo, Michigan, attended by some twenty-five men and women, including Canadian leaders, officers and traveling secretaries. I was the only secretary of foreign birth at that time and also the first Oriental secretary.

Those were the great days of the Student Volunteer Movement. Every campus had its organization of students who hoped to go into foreign service under their respective foreign mission boards. In most colleges they included many of the student leaders. The organization not only helped to set the spiritual tone on each campus but was the forerunner of the current international relations clubs. John R. Mott, Sherwood Eddy and Robert E. Speer were at the height of their leadership. They knew intimately all the great mission fields and their message was authoritative, challenging, deeply moving. They could be counted on to fill the largest auditoriums. They did not call to easy lives but to the hardest kind of adventure, the humblest and most grueling service. And the best of the young manhood and womanhood in the colleges answered.

It would be my responsibility to meet with the college groups, to speak to general student audiences in chapels and convocations, to help recruit new members from whom the various mission boards might choose their candidates for further training. As a part of my own training I received thorough instruction about the problems I would meet in the field and about practical matters of travel. This council meeting stressed spiritual maturity and a living sense of God's guidance, for a secretary could pass on no greater message than she incorporated in her own life. Our leader charged us, "Do you not only believe in the Way, but have you experienced it? The thinking, searching students of this postwar era will confront you with the statement that there are many ways of life—Confucianism, Buddism, Mohammedanism, modernism, humanitarianism, et cetera. How can you verify that Jesus Christ is THE WAY unless you know it from experience?" I could scarcely wait to take our campaign to the front. I thought, some people feel they have to "say something" when called on but I am fortunate because I really have something to say.

9

The First Oriental Traveling Secretary

With a long trip ahead I packed as light a suitcase as possible and carried it along with my brief case. My first assignment was the Lutheran Theological Seminary in Gettysburg. I was met by a professor from the seminary. With a few hours to spare I asked if I might visit the spot where Lincoln had made his memorable address. In psychology class I had memorized his historic speech to ascertain my speed of memorization and length of time of retention but even that had not killed my admiration for it. Standing on the place where the speech was delivered I imagined myself one of the crowd who heard the Great Emancipator and thinking of my own people I prayed that God would help me to aid them to rise above subservience to a despot, to become free, spiritually, politically and economically. An old Korean proverb came to me: "If you lose your teeth, use your gums," but like a modern I thought, "If we don't have any teeth we must make artificial ones."

When I arrived on the platform of the seminary I found that my entire audience was made up of men. Here was I, a young Korean woman, speaking for the first time to men only. I began by saying, "In America when men get

together they call it a stag party." Then without any fore-
thought I made my first play on words in English, "Now
I can see why Korea has been a backward nation. It has
had nothing but stag parties and a country which has only
stag parties soon approaches stagnation." After that, the
audience and I got along fine.

From that time on for the next two years, with the ex-
ception of the summer months, I traveled from the east
coast to the west coast, from north to south, in every state
of the Union and in several provinces of Canada. This
travel kept me packing and unpacking, meeting new faces,
sleeping in college guest rooms, private homes, hotels and
on trains, seeing new scenery and experiencing something
fresh each day. I had some thrilling, exhilarating, tantalizing
and even agonizing experiences. I traveled nearly 100,000
miles, speaking in over three hundred colleges and universities
of all denominations in all states. I never ceased to be deeply
moved by the appreciation of audiences.

Equally moving were the marvels of nature. There was
Niagara Falls spilling about one-half million tons of water
every minute, dropping 165 feet into the gorge, churning
and beating the water and everything in it through the
rocky channel. There was the Grand Canyon nearly three
thousand feet deep with its magnificent colors and overwhelming distances. As I traveled from state to state the in-
dividuality of each intrigued me. The terrain was different;
the main occupations and industries were varied; even the
people were somewhat different. Koreans are Koreans, but
Americans are New Yorkers, or Georgians, or Californians,
or Texans, or what you will. Over-all, however, I felt the
unity of the country—the *United States*.

During my first year with the Student Volunteer Movement, the 1928 presidential election took place, with Herbert
Hoover, Republican, and Alfred E. Smith, Democrat, as the
candidates. It interested me to see the way the people took sides
according to the issue presented. As Election Day approached
arguments waxed hotter and hotter. But the thing that amazed
me most was that after the election the defeated side gave
their full support and co-operation to the winning side and
they all went back to their daily work as if nothing had
happened. "What are the attributes of such a phenomenon?"
I kept asking myself. The answer was old to Americans
but new to me: political education and training, familiarity
with such events every four years, helpful experiences in the
home, in schools and at church for many decades. It reminded me of the verse in the Bible, "An athlete is not
crowned unless he competed according to the rules" (2 Tim.
2:5 r.s.v.). Here many organizations co-operated in teaching an individual the rules of democratic living.

To teach Korean youth how to play a fair, good and clean
game—political or otherwise—in co-operation with others
and to think and choose for themselves as individuals are
two essential prerequisites for a democratic country. Then
we really can authenticate our famous Korean saying, "The
people's will is heaven's will." While we are proud of having
originated such a democratic saying, we have never been
allowed to put it into practice.

On July 24, 1929, President Hoover proclaimed the Kellogg-
Briand Anti-War Treaty under which sixty-two nations pledged
to renounce war as an instrument of national policy. All
over America I met young people who had decided never
to take up arms again even in event of an attack by the

enemy. That was the attitude of the postwar youth toward war—for a time. Then in October the stock market collapsed, plunging America into the worst depression she ever experienced. And yet Christian mission work continued without interruption. Church history has proven again and again that difficult times, including a depression, stimulate the growth of churches and missions, paradoxical as it may appear.

In carrying out my Student Volunteer schedule, personal contacts heartened me all along the way. In North Carolina, for instance, at Duke University, I was introduced by my former dean at Georgia Wesleyan, Walter K. Greene. When I was a student I had given up one of his courses in English literature because he was such a brilliant teacher that I could not follow him. He seemed very pleased that I was able to make a speech in English. It was to me like a homecoming when I returned to my alma mater to speak in the chapel. I was indeed proud to be one of the long line of alumnae of this college, the oldest chartered female college in the United States.

My most unforgettable and dramatic experience was the visit to my blind American sponsor, C. G. Steinhart, and his sister and her husband. They were all my benefactors for they had put me through Ewha High and College in Seoul, and I met them with eighteen years of gratitude. It was Mrs. Whitmore who had sent me my first dollar bill, crisp, narrow and long, with George Washington's picture on it, when I graduated from Ewha High. It was she who sent me the first Bible, King James Version, leather bound, for my college graduation gift. I call her my American mother and she calls me her Korean daughter because she has only three sons and no daughter. Mother Whitmore took me to the Steinharts. Mr. Steinhart was a kindly white-haired gentleman, wearing black glasses because of his blindness. My eyes filled with tears when he put his arms around me and said, "Induk, I wish I could see you face to face but since that is impossible I am grateful that I have a light in my life even greater than physical light; I have the light of God." Then he told me that since I was blessed with two good eyes he expected me to see more than he would be able to see, spiritually as well as physically. Spiritual sight, he felt, was far more important than physical sight. Our meeting was a most satisfying experience for both of us. As I left, he said, "Never forget, Induk, that you have two eyes to see with. See all you can—the sick, the hungry, the lonely and suffering people, and be a light to them."

I had other memorable experiences. In 1929, I was invited to address the Sixtieth Anniversary Convention of the Women's Foreign Missionary Society of the Methodist Church in Columbus, Ohio. There were five to six thousand women, the largest audience I had ever faced. While in Ewha I had learned the history of this organization, how in the early days when in need of funds the women had decided to wear cotton instead of silk dresses. Now they are a powerful group, financing tremendous missionary projects. Had it not been for these women, where would I be today? A second outstanding experience was to speak in a series of meetings for the Florida Chain of Missionary Assemblies held in several cities during the height of the tourist season. Speakers from various mission boards and foreign nationals conducted study classes.

I appreciated being in a semitropical climate in the wintertime. The warmth of the sun, the balmy breezes, the great variety of palm trees, the flame vines carpeting the ground alongside the orange groves, the numerous lakes and beautiful beaches were such a contrast to the great snowdrifts, the enormous icicles, the frost-covered bare trees I had seen in the equally beautiful north. It was remarkable that within the same country people in the south were swimming while in the north people were skiing. One of the sights that amused me in Florida was the sightseers themselves aboard a launch all looking downward. All I could see was the backs of their heads and I could not imagine why they acted so strangely. Then my hostess explained that these people were in a glass-bottomed boat observing underwater life. Soon I too looked down through the crystal pure water and saw to the bottom of Silver Springs.

The people in Florida, including the tourists, showed great interest in missions and gave generously. The first link of the Florida Chain of Missionary Assemblies was started in the twenties at DeLand by Mrs. W. J. Harkness and her churchwomen who felt the need to do something for the tourists in the midst of all the secular amusements. A mission study group was begun with some fine speakers. The program went over so well that other cities joined in and made a chain which today has more than twenty links from Jacksonville to Miami, under the leadership of B. Louise Woodford of St. Petersburg. All the churches unite in sustaining a program on missions attended by thousands every winter.

The result of my being on the Chain was that many individuals in various audiences joined in supporting my future rural work in Korea. This response was not due to any appeal on my part but was a spontaneous reaction after hearing about conditions under which my people lived. However, this support was sponsored and furthered by Miss Woodford and Helen Barrett Montgomery who donated the first one hundred dollars. This audience response created a new project for me and at long last I was going to be able to do something definite for my people.

However, my life as a traveling secretary was not all big meetings or soul-gripping occasions; I addressed hundreds of college groups of all types, large and small, interested or critical. On the whole I found students not only curious about the life of my countrymen but also sympathetic with all of the Orient. They were keenly interested in the sports, occupations, industries and religions of my people as well as in the marriage customs and home life. But whenever I spoke about religion there was always one big question. They held that Oriental people have their own religions, such as Confucianism and Buddhism, which are good enough for their needs. What right have Americans to send Christian missionaries to other countries to urge them to accept our religion?

I thought long and prayed hard in an effort to answer adequately. I realized that these young people had small personal Christian experience and hence no convictions, and that many were antagonistic toward fundamentalism and lenient toward modernism but understood little of either. Why were they so unconvinced of the superiority of Christianity and, with the rest of the world, so ready to acknowledge some other leadership? In Europe about that time the defeated German youth were marching under the Nazi banner, the Italians were marching under the Fascist banner, the Russian Revolution was well under way with the proletarian youth marching under the Communist banner. In Japan, too, the youth were marching under the militaristic banner. Each group in its own way was attempting to find some solution for the world's problems. American college youth were feeling this wave of unrest and were beginning to talk of the unequal distribution of wealth and wondering why it was permitted. They felt that politically and economically Christianity had proven inadequate. They told me that my people must work out their own solutions with the help of their own religions. "We have Christianity and just see what a mess we have made," they said, pointing out the dire social conditions and grave race problems with which they were confronted.

Knowing Christianity from personal experience and having felt its power to uplift, my answer was as simple as A B C and as profound as the fathomless ocean. Being a Christian convert I knew that Christianity is the religion of love. Through love one can expand and develop to the fullest degree. Christianity recognizes the personal value of the individual so that no matter who he is or to what rank he belongs he is valuable in the eyes of God, his creator.

I explained to them about our religions in Korea. Shamanism, which is polytheistic, had evidently been practiced by the original tribes when Korea was founded by Tangun (gun—sovereign or prince). The Shamanists believe that spirits reside in places and objects, such as mountains, rivers, old trees, imagelike rocks, deep wells and wide caves. They believe that there are two kinds of spirits—benevolent and vindictive. Sickness, death and the many miseries experienced in one's life are supposed to be caused by the bad spirits; therefore they should be placated in order to stop such mischief. A priestess is hired to give a propitiatory performance, consisting of songs, dances and instrumental music; also food and clothing are offered to the angry spirits. Some of the performers are very skilled, and can stand barefoot on the razorlike edge of a sword, or dance on the rim of a large basin filled brimful of water without spilling a drop. Living under such a religion, surrounded by revengeful spirits, one cannot help but feel a constant fear, heavy suspicions and a dreadful uncertainty. One never knows who will be next to be struck by mad spirits. Often a normal accident will be interpreted as evidence of an evil spirit, and the person involved will be overwhelmed by mumbo-jumbo incantations and rites in order to rid himself of the possessing demons. What chance does he have for a normal recovery? I am gratified that this cult is on the wane as enlightenment reaches out across our peninsula.

Buddhism was founded in India in 560 B.C. by Gautama Buddha, the Enlightened One. Raised a prince with all the advantages of wealth and culture, he nevertheless became interested in finding life's true meaning and gave up his sumptuous way of life, even leaving his wife and son for some years while he went forth into the wilderness to find the inner peace which comes with discovery of life's meaning. He endured temptations and privations and eventually felt his way to the heart of the matter, a realization that God is in and through all but that to approach Him, to share His holy nature, one must have no addictions to life, no self-will, no desire to be anything apart from God. Buddha then returned to the world, gathered disciples around him, including his own wife, and served the people until he died. But he never succeeded in making his followers feel that God was a father, that He cared terrifically for the welfare of each individual; nor did he sense the importance to others of each ordinary individual's holy life expressed in service to others, meeting the needs of others as if they were one's own needs. Nor did he pass on his own knowledge with power, with a sense of victory, with the affirmation that "all things are possible to them that love God." And so Buddhism has become a passive religion with its adherents seeking their own personal salvation through contemplation and withdrawal from daily life. The Hinduism from which it sprang still persists in a multiplicity of gods and a background of constant taboos and sacrifices. Moreover, Buddha, the central figure, and Kwan-yin, Goddess of Mercy, must constantly be petitioned for favors rather than for power and a sharing of their wise and loving will for mankind.

Buddhism reached Korea in A.D. 372 and played an important part in the fortunes of the dynasties, the priests often influencing political life to the point of corrupting officials, with constant disaster. Nevertheless they were responsible for building beautiful Buddhist temples and pagodas, for casting clear and appealing bells, for making sublime images of Buddha in gold, bronze, marble or granite, for producing exquisite wood carvings and painting gorgeous murals. Yet having become primarily a religion of withdrawal and negation, Buddhism did not meet my mother's needs, or my needs, or those of my poeple. What had Buddhism to offer to an impoverished people under the Japanese occupation? Buddhism does not think in terms of personal problems and hence it offers no solution, neither claiming nor evidencing the power of the Holy Spirit.

Confucianism is a moral system centered around two virtues,

duty and benevolence. In the sixth century B.C. China was in a state of chaos, with poverty and lawlessness abounding. In changing from the old feudal system the people needed a new set of values to which they could cling and with which to rebuild their lives. Confucius saw this need. He declared that social well-being was possible only if each individual performed his social obligations. These obligations were grouped under five headings: ruler and subject, parent and child, husband and wife, elder brother and younger brother, friend and friend. The ruler must be benevolent and the subject must be loyal; the parent must be kind and the child display filial duty; the husband must be righteous and his wife submissive; the elder brother must be gentle and the younger brother obedient; friend must be faithful to friend. In each of these relationships there were set proprieties to be observed and conventions accordingly established. Under these five groups only friends were on the same level; in the other four, the subordinate must be submissive. There was no opportunity for the subordinate to come to independent judgment and full stature. Realizing that duty alone would not give satisfaction, benevolence was added, but it lacked the activating force of Christianity which makes each Christian his brother's keeper.

Until Christianity came, the average Korean had no ties uniting him with God. He also had a very limited understanding as to who was his neighbor. Through Jesus, he learned of God's love, a stupendous conception of a Divine Ruler. Through Jesus, he learned the way of life and the inconsequence of death. Through Jesus, he laid hold on a living power, the guidance of the Holy Spirit. These are all dynamic factors which release an individual's full nature, give him hope, determination, aspiration, give him *life*. I could speak with conviction about these fundamentals of religion. I could also tell these young people what Christianity had given my mother and me and I did my best to lead them to know the power of Christianity for all the people of the world.

During my two years of travel for the Student Volunteer Movement I took courses at Columbia University Summer School and in the fall of 1930 I attended Teachers College for a full semester, staying at International House. More than sixty nationalities were represented there, and every shade of skin. Each individual came from a different cultural background with the purpose of preparing himself with specialized knowledge in order to return and help better the living standards of his own people. I got to know my fellow students, learning of their hopes, aspirations and problems, as well as to airing some of my own opinions! Students often took turns in presenting programs which set forth some aspect of their culture or needs. Outstanding personalities from various countries were brought to the International House family to address us. Among them was Rabindranath Tagore, Hindu poet, dramatist and Nobel Prize winner in 1913. He was a large and dignified man. During his lecture he recited some of his own poetry, and his calm, serene manner was to me a symbol of the finest and best in Indian culture.

In the back of my mind I kept pondering what my next step should be. I felt a definite need to return to Korea. But I wished to travel home by a different route, realizing that I might never have another opportunity to see Europe. However, my reason for wanting to return to Korea through Europe was more than just wishing to go on a sightseeing tour. I felt definitely the postwar tension and restlessness among the overseas students at International House and I wanted to see for myself what was happening abroad in that important part of the world. So I prayed and worked toward that end.

IO

On Three Continents

In the late fall while attending a week-end conference I met Margaret Read of England who was one of the speakers. As we talked together I mentioned that I would like to visit Europe on my way home. After she had heard me speak, she told me she wished I could come to England to address the college students there, as they had never heard a Korean. She said she herself was planning to return to England after the conference and would be glad to contact the leaders of the Student Christian Movement in Great Britain and Ireland. A month later I received a letter telling me that everything had been arranged; they would like to have me come for three months. Overjoyed with this timely engagement, I accepted. I was to receive my M.A. degree about February 1, so I arranged to sail on the S.S. Bremen on February 10. Four and a half years previous I had arrived in San Francisco as a steerage passenger. Now I was returning home in a tourist cabin, via Europe, leaving behind many friends, and taking with me a new knowledge and many living memories. Surely America had given me a great deal.

After five days of smooth sailing we arrived in Southampton where many British battleships rode in the harbor, symbol of British naval supremacy. Going through customs I heard a new pronunciation of English. It was very interesting to me to listen to these Britishers talk. Train accommodations were different from any I had previously known, with compartments carrying four or six passengers, each compartment with its own door. Passengers did not chat informally as they did in America; they spoke only when directly addressed.

At Waterloo Station I was met by Miss Read who took me in a taxi to her home some distance away. It was Sunday and I noticed that all the stores were closed and the streets very quiet, even though London was a great metropolitan city. Ordinarily I do not eat much bread but that evening at supper I tasted the best homemade bread I had ever eaten, as well as English tea and plum pudding.

The next day my friend taught me how to use English money of all denominations, and this was doubly difficult for me as I had to calculate it in American valuation first and then in Korean. She also provided me with a map of London, including the tube systems, and told me that I would have two weeks for sightseeing before beginning my itinerary. She took me into the main thoroughfare of London and showed me the tubes, trolleys and buses, and the station where I should get off to go to her home—which was to be my home while I was in London. I was advised, also, to approach a bobby (policeman) if I got lost. One rainy day, going into the city during the rush hour, I had to cross a very wide street. There was no light signal and the bobby who was directing traffic saw me waiting. Stopping the traffic he came to me, took me by the arm, and conducted me across the thoroughfare. As the heavy traffic began to move again, I smiled as I thought of all this activity being stopped just for me—a lone Korean woman in the middle of London. Because of my happy experience while in England I hold a very warm place in my heart for all Britishers.

I knew that there were two Korean gentlemen in London at this time, one a student, D. S. Chang, working for his Ph.D. degree, and the other, S. S. Kim, president of Posung College of Seoul, on a tour. After I had got in touch with them, Mr. Chang, whom I had known previously in New York, took the time to show me around. In my roaming about the city I found the stores well stocked with all sorts of merchandise.

Miss Read introduced me to many of her interesting friends. Four o'clock tea, observed both in the home and at school, offered a time of relaxed discussion. We also found time to attend the cinema and to see *The Barretts of Wimpole Street, Joan of Arc* and *Strange Interlude* on the legitimate stage.

My speaking tour began at the girls' college in Cambridge where I saw many traditional customs still being followed, as for instance, in the dining hall the use of an elevated table for teachers. I visited twenty-three colleges and universities in England, Wales, Scotland and Ireland. The meetings I addressed on campuses were sponsored by three groups—The Student Christian Movement, The Society of Geography and The League of Nations. Generally speaking, English students seemed very reserved but when they asked a question it was well thought out. They were more mature and also inclined to be more political-minded than the free and unaffected American youth. No doubt their attitude was due in part to their interests in their world-wide colonies.

When I went to the School of Geography at the University of Liverpool, I was almost overcome to see the maps of Korea made by the students. One of the professors said, "Mrs. Pahk, we want you to feel at home. Just look at all these maps." Surrounded by such reminders of my homeland, I spoke to the students feelingly on "My Country and My People," after which I was bombarded with questions. One student said, "We tried to get some references on Korea in the library but found very little. What we did find had been written by the Japanese, from their point of view. Now we would like to have your opinion on several questions. What do you think of the Japanese policy? Are things getting better in Korea? How is the farming situation?" et cetera.

After my lecture another student came to me and said, "Auh, Mrs. Pahk, you doan't speak English atall."

With much amusement, I inquired, "What do I speak, then?"

He replied, "You speak American."

Mischievously I concluded, "I don't speak American, either. I speak Korean-American," and in typically English fashion he answered, "Right-o!"

At one church in Wales a young girl brought a Korean Bible to me as a gift. It had been printed by the British Bible Tract Society in Seoul. I opened the Korean Bible and in our tongue read the parable of the prodigal son. Then the girl who had presented the Bible read the parable in Welsh. Finally the minister read it in English. We ended our service with fervent prayers for England and Korea. I sent the Bible to my daughters in Seoul.

Back in London again, I attended a session of Parliament. The Labor party, headed by J. Ramsay MacDonald, was in power at that time. The whole bewigged procession, formal and reminiscent of history, was impressive and the freedom of speech exhibited on the floor surprised and excited me, especially the speech made by Margaret Bonfield who was then the Minister of Labor. The way questions were hurled at her and her quick retorts reminded me of a tennis match. To me a woman in the role of statesman was something new. I knew that the suffrage movement had originated in England and found that it still had plenty of modern exponents.

Facing homeward, I wished to visit other European countries. One day during a conference I had met a lady from Belgium who was on the board of the Y.W.C.A. in Brussels. When she learned that I had never been in Belgium she asked, "Wouldn't you like to come to Brussels and speak to our students?" And before I could answer she told me that she would plan to have me for a three-day speaking tour, assuring me that my expenses would be taken care of. Without hesitation I agreed and on May 15 I left London, crossed the Channel, and took a train to Brussels where I was met and taken to the Y.W.C.A.

The next evening there was a large public meeting in one of the churches, sponsored by the Y.W.C.A. As I spoke in English my address was interpreted into French. I was told that I was the first Korean speaker they had ever heard. These people had suffered much at the hands of the Germans in World War I and naturally understood how we Koreans had fared under the domination of the Japanese. I was greatly gratified by their words of encouragement and by their display of spirit.

My Belgian hostess took me around the next day and pointed out places which had been destroyed by the Germans but were already restored by the people. She said, "My country is on the highway between Germany and France. You Koreans understand what that means." As I saw the forward and upward look of this wonderful nation I thought how God blesses those who carry on courageously in spite of all adversities.

My next jump was Denmark. The chief reason for going to Denmark was to observe how the Danish Folk High Schools and Co-operatives were operated. Before leaving England I had contacted Peter Manniche who was head of the International People's College in Elsinore where an experiment of the Danish system of adult education was being carried out. At a time when their country was almost on the verge of bankruptcy and had few natural resources, the Danes had decided to do something about their predicament and so they began to produce and distribute their products by co-operative effort. Their success was tremendous. Since in many ways their situation was analogous to ours in Korea, I wanted to learn all I could about their methods. On my way to Copenhagen by train I saw many evidences of their achievement—horses, pigs, cows and poultry in the green peaceful fields. This was in May, 1931.

From Elsinore where Dr. Manniche met me, I could see Sweden across the bay and almost felt as if I had returned to my birthplace in Chinnampo because of the mountains and the sea. When I arrived at the school there were about forty-five Danish students for the summer session and some fifteen visitors from England, the Continent and the United States. I was the only Oriental. The whole school appeared to be delighted to have a visitor from the Far East. Dr. Manniche asked me to sign the guest book, pointing to the signatures of some recent Korean visitors. They were all personal friends— two gentlemen from the Seoul Y.M.C.A. and a lady from Ewha College. It warmed my heart to know that occasionally my path crossed that of my countrymen.

Singing appeared to be one of the outstanding courses in the Folk High Schools. Folk songs were sung lustily at meals, between courses, after meals, before and after classes, and at bedtime, all of the students knowing about a hundred songs of hope and inspiration. "A singing people never dies" . . . "While they sing they become one" were their slogans. Gymnastics also figured prominently in the curriculum.

One night was designated as guest night and the townspeople were invited to meet the guests of the school. Nearly a hundred came on their bicycles which are their main means of transportation. Everyone enjoyed the singing, gymnastics and short speeches, after which folk dancing completed the program, followed by refreshments of black coffee, fruit and cookies. By this time I was thoroughly convinced that the Danish people were alive and progressive. Denmark was the first country I visited which had not been affected by the war, having remained neutral.

For two weeks I attended courses on co-operative marketing and international problems as related to the Danish people, classes conducted almost entirely by the discussion method in which all participated. The class was required to visit various farms, co-operatives and private homes in order to gain a proper perspective, and I learned that Denmark supplied most of the breakfast tables of London.

My first destination after leaving Denmark was Berlin. As I visited the campus of the University of Berlin I was impressed by the stubborn determination of the young people to overcome the defeat they had suffered in World War I. In England I had found the students reserved and confident; in Denmark they had been keenly interested in their own economic situation; in Germany they seemed bitter and resentful toward the Treaty of Versailles and bound to achieve, as a kind of vindication. As I traveled about the city and surrounding area I saw great activity among the youth who dressed in uniforms which somewhat resembled those of the Boy Scouts and seemed always to be marching under the leadership of Hitler. I saw model buildings called "Twenty-first Century" models, indicating the forward look of the people. One felt the spirit of determination which dominated Germany in 1931.

On the spur of the moment, I decided to go to Moscow but when I applied at the Russian Embassy for a tourist visa, I was told that they could not give me any assurance as to the length of time it would take to get my credentials. When I asked why, they said that was their business and not mine. I said that I would take a chance. And so I applied and waited three weeks, going to the visa office almost every day. Finally one morning I was told that I had been granted permission to go on to Russia the following Monday.

I boarded the train coming from Paris. At eight o'clock in the morning we stopped for half an hour at the Warsaw station which was crowded with working people. As I walked back and forth on the platform I thought of the suffering of the Polish people. Poland, too, had been partitioned several times and yet the people never ceased their efforts to regain their independence. How well our Korean saying, "Uttermost devotion moves the heavens," applied to the Poles. At last at the end of World War I they were independent. Poland and Ireland were our models in pursuing our Korean independence. But when I arrived at the border of Russia I felt tension just from looking at the border guards and I left Poland with an uneasy feeling. When we reached the Russian city Niegorele, credentials and luggage were carefully examined and I changed my traveler's checks into Russian rubles. We were moved onto a Russian train and I was assigned to a compartment with a young German woman who was going to Moscow to join her husband. The second day while the train stopped at Minsk for a half hour we got off to take a bit of exercise. A train from the opposite direction also had a stopover period and to my complete astonishment I met Dr. and Mrs. F. I. Johnson, whom I had known in Florida while on the Florida Chain of Missions trip. They had been to Moscow and were returning. We had time enough to drink a cup of coffee in their compartment and made the most of our precious minutes together.

Riding through the Russian countryside I was surprised to see the poverty and the many thatch-roofed houses in contrast to the domes and spires of the Russian Orthodox churches. I was interested to find a quaint practice in effect along the railway. When the train stopped at wayside villages, farm women were on the platform to sell homemade bread, cooked chicken and fresh fruits to passengers. Many who could not afford the luxury of dining-car service took advantage of these offerings. Others carried box lunches. There were six other tourists on our train: two couples, one from South America and the other from Germany; one man from France and another from Italy. I was again the only Oriental. When we arrived in Moscow we were met by a Russian guide and taken to a hotel. A multiplicity of placards printed in red were spread everywhere. It was early afternoon, and we were advised that our tour would begin the next morning after breakfast which would be served at ten o'clock. Next day at noon the guard made his appearance and we started out.

Of course the "glories" of the Communist regime were constantly brought to our attention. When we were taken to the tomb in Red Square where the embalmed Lenin was shown, we had to wait in line because there was so large a mob ahead of us. We visited a day nursery in which the government took care of children while their parents worked in periods of five days followed by one day of rest. The government did not acknowledge a "Sunday"; they had their own system of weeks. In parks speakers constantly indoctrinated their listeners with Red propaganda and ritual. Newspapers and illustrated bulletins extolling the Communist way of life were plastered on every available surface and laborers came between shifts for the occasional bit of news sandwiched in between these Red items.

Motion pictures were extensively utilized for propaganda; the people paid to be thus propaganized but the admission fee was small. Religion was ridiculed whenever possible but science was glorified along with communism. Marriage and divorce could be speedily transacted. We also visited a prison and an institution where former prostitutes could earn an honest livelihood by making hosiery.

As I moved about this great city I was horrified by the gaunt appearance of the people and by the breadlines for which each family was given tickets to purchase bread if the breadwinner had worked according to schedule. Soviet Russia was then in the midst of her Five Year Plan. The men wore no hats as they had none. About three o'clock every morning, the streets were dominated by youth groups singing and shouting in their great rumbling trucks. Stalin's pictures were everywhere. Food was scarce. Our schedule called for lunch at three with dinner at nine but frequently the meal was delayed while food was located. We should be very patient with the common people of Russia for all they have gone through. It was a real relief to get away from such an atmosphere but at the same time I felt much concern, realizing that some great evil force was working against a free society.

En route to Vienna I changed trains at the Russian border and again in Warsaw. During the night the train crossed two border lines, Poland to Czechoslovakia and Czechoslovakia to Austria. Each time this happened customs officials came into the compartment, examined passports and luggage, and asked about each passenger's destination and reason for traveling. I noted that this interrogation was made by a number of officials, each doing some very small part; one examined the passport, another stamped it, still another certified the luggage, and so on. When I asked one harmless-looking Czech official why they had so many men doing little jobs, he replied with a twinkle in his eye, "That's the way we solve the unemployment problem." But behind the twinkle in his eye there was another story. Many stormy days were ahead for his country because of her Sudetenland on the German border. I wondered what the future of this twelve-year-old republic would be.

We arrived in Vienna in the early morning. Since I had just one day to spend, I decided to take a regular sightseeing tour to see the Blue Danube, the palaces, museums and other sights. A couple from California in typical American fashion invited me to have dinner with them at the hotel. Then on to Switzerland, Europe's winter playground, home of the League of Nations and other international organizations. Early the next morning the snow-covered Alps were illumined by the rising sun. I had made no contacts with anyone but had no difficulty in finding a room in a nice pension in Geneva. A parade, with colorfully dressed marchers and excellent music, and a showing of merchandise and fine produce from the twenty-two cantons of Switzerland gave me an unexpected opportunity to get a bird's-eye view of the people and their products. Switzerland and Denmark were the only countries in Europe where I found the people enjoying life.

Although the Swiss have no national language but use French, German or Italian depending upon the locale, their spirit was unmistakably *Swiss*. This tiny country has succeeded for centuries in remaining neutral and keeping free from war even though surrounded by powerful neighbors. Wherever I went I asked about this tradition and the reply was invariably the same, "We train our people to defend their country but not to meddle in the affairs of other countries."

The trip from Switzerland to Italy through the Rhone Valley to Milan was a picturesque ride, with turquoise waterfalls adding sparkle and splendor. From Switzerland to Italy we went through the Simplon Pass, twelve and one-half miles of tunnel through the Alps. Halfway through the Pass, policed by Swiss and Italian guards, the Swiss electric train stopped and each passenger's passport and suitcases were carefully checked. As I rode under these famous mountains I remembered how Napoleon and his army marched over them afoot and it seemed incredible what great changes science, engineering and time had wrought.

In Milan I changed trains for Venice, arriving at eight-thirty in the evening. My hotel room faced the waterway street and I felt as though I were on an unmoving steamer. The next day I went forth in a gondola while two gondoliers with broad-brimmed hats and bright sashes propelled the boat and pointed out the Bridge of Sighs, San Marco Piazza with St. Mark's Cathedral and its thousands of pigeons about which I had read in Korea.

In Rome I was met by a member of the staff of the Y.W.C.A. and I was greatly relieved when I saw her. It is fine to travel alone but I think I felt a bit homesick, or lonesome. I stayed at the Y.W.C.A. while doing Rome and of all the things I saw in that city three sights stand out in my memory. First, the catacombs. As we tourists took lighted candles and went down several flights of steps and through long damp corridors, we talked of the loyalty of the early Christians during the Roman persecution. The Christian religion they had preserved came eventually even to me, as a little child in far-off Korea. Second in importance was St. Peter's Cathedral, a magnificent marble structure into which artists, architects and artisans had put their intellect, their bodies, their blood and even a bit of their souls. Third, and perhaps the most appealing in a personal way, was the little church called Quo Vadis where I saw a footprint supposed to be that of Christ. Legend tells us that when Nero burned Rome and placed the blame on the Christians, Peter became frightened and was running away when he met Christ. Peter asked him, *"Quo vadis?"* meaning "Whither goest thou?" and then Jesus told Peter that he was returning to Rome to be crucified again. Whether the story is true or the footprint authentic does not matter too much. It was a paramount experience for me just to be there.

On the way to Naples by train I noticed other passengers looking eagerly out of the windows, so I too looked, and saw dense clouds of smoke pouring from the top of a mountain which I knew must be Vesuvius. One could not help but speculate as to this volcano's tremendous power and unpredictable activity and of course the pitiful helplessness of man against such forces.

Throughout all of my jaunts and visits while in Rome, I was conscious of many cautious remarks extolling Il Duce, constant praises of him as a man and of his accomplishments for his people. I was impressed by the youth movements which had been rising under the dictatorship of Mussolini and the Fascist party ever since their march on Rome in October, 1922. As my stay in Italy was drawing to a close I was debating whether or not to take the northern Mediterranean route at additional expense when an unexpected incident settled the question. In my mail, which had been forwarded to me at the Y.W.C.A. in Naples, was a letter from America containing a gift of one hundred dollars. I happily decided to take the northern route.

When I arrived on board the Italian freighter there were four Americans already on deck—the Barnett Sisters, Leah and Gladys, another young girl and a young man. All four were American Jews bound for a visit to Palestine. As our boat passed through the Corinth canal I was reminded of Paul's epistles to the Corinthians. For me this territory was filled with Biblical characters and happenings. We arrived in Athens before breakfast and the five of us went ashore where we visited the old weather-beaten ruins, mute testimony to the civilization which had once flourished among these hills. A visit to the amphitheater where the Olympic games had originated and where the youth of the world had competed in 1906, created within me a desire to have my own countrymen take part in these Olympic contests, which they have since done with considerable distinction. This was the country where Socrates and Plato once lived and taught, but more—this was the place where Paul delivered his famous sermon to the Athenians: "Yet he is not far from each one of us, for 'in him we live and move and have our being'" (Acts 17:27-28, r.s.v.).

Our next long stopover was Constantinople, the name of which has since been changed to Istanbul. This city is situated on two continents—one side in Europe and the other in Asia. The many quaint mosques with their domes and minarets looked to me like soldiers with helmets and guns. We noticed that the Mohammedan women had discarded their veils and felt that something modern must be stirring in Turkey since it had become a republic in 1923. President Mustafa Kemal had already carried out extensive programs in reforms, modernization and industrialization. Our guide noticed our great interest in the women's veils and told us, "You know a person cannot see much with a veil on. Now the entire country can see far and wide." He explained further that following the unveiling of their faces the women had shown great eagerness to learn. A little later on one of the party asked him if Turkish men still had many wives. He smiled but made no answer, and after a few minutes of thought, asked me," How about the Oriental men?"

We visited the great bazaar where merchants sold all sorts of merchandise, sitting on the ground to conduct their business. In such a mart East indeed meets West. The mosques, including St. Sophia, with their basins for ceremonial washing before worship, displayed incredible mosaic art work. As I stood on a hill gazing down on this great city with the Black Sea on one side and the Mediterranean on the other, I could understand why it was looked upon enviously by so many countries: for Russia it would provide a gateway to the sea; for Germany, an entrance to the treasures of Asia; for Great Britain, a trade route to her Eastern possessions; for Greece it was Byzantium to which she claimed a historical right.

From Beirut, Syria, formerly a Turkish province which had been under French mandate since World War I, we took a trip to Damascus. My Jewish traveling companions joined me in hiring a Moslem guide with a motor car, and after driving us up, up, up, he stopped in the clouds on the top of a mountain and said, "Do you know what happened here? Which one of you is a Christian?" I indicated that I was a Christian and he directed his next piece of information to me. "This is where Saul's name was changed to Paul. Here Saul was blinded by God's presence and from here he went on to Damascus." He told us that although he was a Mohammedan he believed this report for anyone looking about him here would be struck by God's voice through his conscience if he were engaged in anything wrong.

On the way down the mountain our party stopped at a little house where a man was selling water carried in a goatskin, and for a price he opened the corner of the container and gave each of us a drink. We then went on down to the street called "Straight." As we poked about we ran across a food very similar to the pancakes which we have in America and Korea. We bought some and they were good. Such a little thing as this made us feel much less strange.

On my return trip to Beirut I saw a man riding on a horse while a woman walked behind. I wondered whether they were husband and wife. Another unforgettable scene was a group of Bedouins with colorful turbans and flowing robes moving in caravans with their camels led by a small donkey. These men looked fierce but fascinating. Also the full, flowing robes worn by both men and women had an Oriental flavor. Typically nomad, their leisureliness with small concern for the passage of time indicated a philosophical rather than a scientific outlook on life. Barren, dusty fields showed a lack of productiveness. In a rather far-fetched way, these Bedouins reminded me of Confucian scholars who also have a total lack of economic responsibility.

Our next stop was Haifa which had been under British mandate since World War I. Here my Jewish friends and I left the steamer for good and hired a taxi to Jerusalem. Passing Mount Carmel we stopped at Nazareth. I had been eager to step on this sacred soil and could scarcely believe that my dream was at last being fulfilled. We visited a carpenter shop where we saw tools similar to those which Jesus used in his trade. Here in this very town he had put his tools away and closed the door and started out on his ministry. I visualized this action with such intensity that I could hear my own pulse beating. As I saw children playing in the streets I thought what a different world this would be if they saw and felt what Jesus saw and felt when he lived there. Women carrying water jugs on their shoulders, and the heavy millstones grinding meal, reminded me of home.

When we arrived in Jerusalem I stayed with my Jewish companions in an orthodox Jewish home. On Friday at sundown they began their Sabbath. I knew that the Mohammedans observed their Sabbath on Friday while the Christians observed Sunday, and so each closed his store or place of business on his own holy day. The religion of the proprietor could be ascertained by the day on which his place of business was closed.

We visited the Jordan River and the Dead Sea, but since my fellow travelers were not interested in the Sea of Galilee, we had to skip it, much to my regret. But there was Jericho, scene of the parable of the good Samaritan; Bethany, with its flat-roofed houses like the home of Mary and Martha and their brother Lazarus; Bethlehem, with its hillsides still giving pasture to sheep tended by shepherds. When shown the spot reputed to be the birthplace of Jesus, I was deeply moved and did not really care whether it was the exact spot or not. For me the climax was the garden of Gethsemane where the Son of God committed himself to his Father's will.

The building of Tel Aviv by the Jews had already begun

with the draining of the swamps and the erection of modern buildings, including a hospital. The Zionist movement to create a Jewish homeland in Palestine and the efforts of Great Britain to establish Palestine as a Jewish country in accordance with the Balfour Declaration were meeting much opposition from the Arabs. Indeed, tension between the Jews and Arabs was so strong even then that a mere tourist was conscious of it.

Leaving my Jewish friends in Jerusalem I traveled alone by train to Cairo. Soon after the trip began we noticed that the passenger cars had stopped and looking about for the reason, we saw the locomotive traveling ahead by itself. In some way it had become detached. The passengers scrambled out in excitement, screaming and yelling and waving their arms madly until finally the engineer realized that his locomotive was traveling awfully light and stopped, backed up, and attached it again to the rest of the cars. The little stations in the desert really surprised me; sitting alone in the middle of nowhere they looked sadly forlorn. The trip from Jerusalem to Cairo took about twelve hours and I marveled again as I remembered the forty years of vicissitudes which the Jews had experienced under the leadership of Moses when he led them out of bondage in Egypt and up to the Promised Land. How we Koreans venerated Moses!

Arriving in Cairo I headed for the Y.W.C.A. where I met an American missionary who had worked in Seoul and was returning to America via Europe. Together we visited the Sphinx and the Pyramids which were immensely larger than they seemed in their pictures. From Cairo I went by train to Port Said where I took an English P & O steamer through the Suez Canal. The parching winds blowing off the desert made the steamer unbearably hot. Once we reached the Indian Ocean, however, it was much cooler and the trip across to Bombay was correspondingly pleasant.

Arriving at Bombay on August 15, my predominant impressions here were of colors, caste and culture. An old culture. The monsoons, when water comes down by bucketfuls, had been followed by extreme heat which was almost unendurable. I was surprised to note how the workers carried their burdens on their heads just as the women of Korea do. Newspapers reported that Mahatma Gandhi had just left this very port to attend the Round Table Conference in London.

Desiring to see the Taj Mahal I took a train to Agra and found the countryside beautiful following the wet season. The great variety of native dress represented a corresponding variety of religions. The mass of people presented a tremendous man-power potential. If only these hordes of people could become enlightened and provided with some means of working out their livelihood, what a changed country India would be. When the train stopped the untouchables came in to sweep and clean the cars. Later I visited Holman Institute, a mission school for untouchables where the slogan was "You were born low caste but you can live and die as Sons of God." What more powerful sword than this? The name of Gandhi was on everyone's lips, and this was the first time I had heard one man's name mentioned so frequently since leaving Russia and Italy. By this fact I suspected that a great force was moving here, too.

I found the Taj Mahal to be as reputed, surely the most beautiful temple in the world. Built in the seventeenth century by Shah-Jahan as a memorial to his favorite queen, it had been erected on a flat marble platform on the bank of the Jumna River by twenty thousand workmen who labored for twenty years at a cost of twenty million dollars. Made of white marble, its interior is inlaid with mosaics of precious stones, including jasper, carnelian and lapis lazuli. It is indeed a dream transformed into marble! An inscription above the doorway reads, "TO THE MEMORY OF AN UNDYING LOVE." On the advice of the guide I repeated the phrase aloud. The sound went up and up against the high ceiling and rebounded . . . "TO THE MEMORY OF AN UNDYING LOVE . . . UNDYING LOVE . . . UNDYING LOVE . . ." giving such a sweet quality to my voice that I was quite awed by it. What irony, I thought, that this exquisite memorial was built to honor a beloved Indian queen while the lot of Indian women in general is indifference and neglect.

The next stop was Lucknow, home of Isabella Thoburn College, the first college for women in the Orient, established by the Methodist Board of Foreign Missions. The principal of the college met my train and took me to the guest room. Somewhat later I addressed the girls in the high school and they presented me with a beautiful sari in appreciation of the scholarship given by my alma mater in Seoul. I also addressed three hundred men students in this city and was told that no other Oriental woman had ever spoken there. They were greatly interested in politics and since they were under British domination, as Korea was under Japan, they listened eagerly to what I had to say. In open discussion they agreed that the road to independence was to make every fellow countryman free and independent in thought and they understood that unless they did this for themselves they would not succeed. Since Gandhi had gone to England they were on their toes and when I told them that the Koreans had conducted a nonaggressive resistance movement in 1919 against the Japanese, they were much impressed.

From Lucknow I went by train to Calcutta where I was met by an American missionary who took me to the Lee Memorial

Institute for underprivileged Indian girls. She and her husband had lost five of their six children in a landslide at their summer home in the mountains and had established this Institute as a memorial to them. When I was ready to leave Calcutta, Mrs. Lee took me in her carriage to the steamer. On board we went to my stateroom and prayed together. She prayed for my safety as I journeyed homeward and I was wonderfully heartened. This woman proved herself strong in courage and faith as well as being full of good works.

The boat stopped at Rangoon for a day where I visited the indescribably elaborate Buddhist temple, Shwe Dagon. The way the worshipers burned candles reminded me of the Buddhist temples in my country. The women's dress seemed a combination of the Japanese kimono topped by a Chinese jacket while the coiffure looked like the traditional Korean gentleman's hat minus the brim. Here women seemed more free and active, as independent as the men, something I had never before seen in Oriental women. I also saw some Burmese men wearing topknots similar to the old-style hairdress of Korean men. Little did I think when I was there that Burma was to become a key battleground in World War II.

On September 2 I arrived in Singapore. I was now not far from the equator and it was very, very hot. The harbor was buzzing with activity, steamers coming and going, commercial vessels traveling between Eastern Asia, India and Europe. Singapore was also a refueling station and we could see the naval coaling depot for Great Britain, well defended by forts and batteries. I stayed at the Mission School for Girls and addressed the students there. Having never seen snow, these young folks asked eager questions about how it looked and felt. I fully realized the sacrifices missionaries had made in leaving their homes in a temperate climate to come here; only between midnight and dawn was there any degree of comfort. Life was made bearable only by pulling down the shades after lunch, taking a rest period, followed by a bath and tea. Then it was possible to work until a late dinner. My missionary friend drove me into the Malayan jungles for fifteen or twenty miles where I saw houses built on stilts. In Korea we had similar buildings on the melon fields where the men and boys watched their crops to protect them from marauders. The predominance of rubber trees left no doubt as to the importance of the rubber industry here.

From Singapore I took a P & O steamer to Hong Kong which had been occupied by the British since 1841. The Hong Kong harbor on the Canton River is considered one of the most beautiful harbors in the world but it lies in a typhoon belt and there had been such a huge storm recently that a high tide, forty feet above normal, had cast a large ocean liner on the shore. Also a piece had been sheared off a mountain, making a new cliff, mute testimony to the power of the storm.

As the steamer docked, I was kept busy watching the houseboats which literally swarmed in the harbor. Often they accommodated families made up of several generations and as I watched the families gathered about their evening meal happily eating with chopsticks, holding their bowls of rice, laughing and talking together, I was convinced that what people have of this world's goods does not necessarily make happiness. These boat people made a living by transporting cargoes from the vessels to the docks. Hong Kong, as a main artery of commerce for China as well as for eastern Asia and as a British naval base, was full of fascination for me.

The next stop was Shanghai. Here one of my Ewha students,

Kim Meedo, entertained me. She had married and was the mother of two girls and a boy, the older girl my namesake. Meedo owned a factory with a dozen or more Korean and Chinese women working for her, making chenille bedspreads which were sold in the International Settlement. She was unusually enterprising and progressive and I admired her initiative. Under her guidance I traveled the well-planned and well-kept streets, visiting the miles of wharves, factories and shops. Chinese silks with their unexcelled quality and beauty attracted me greatly, I must admit, as did the fine restaurants with their great variety of delicious foods. Here there was good food aplenty and yet hordes of poverty-stricken people abounded on every hand. This vast inequality bothered me greatly every time I met up with it—which was practically all the time after we left Europe.

In the Chinese section we saw young men making speeches on the street and my friend, who understood Chinese, told me that they were indignantly talking against the Japanese invasion in Manchuria which had occurred about a week previous. Sensing the tenseness of the situation, my friend advised that if I planned to go home I had best leave as soon as possible. Taking her advice I boarded a train for Peiping, stopping en route at Nanking to visit Gingling College, a mission college for girls. Here I was happily surprised at the independence and matter-of-factness displayed by the Chinese girl students and I foresaw in them the hope of China. These educated young women would become wives and mothers and use their new-found power and influence to advantage.

Arriving in Peiping a week after the Manchurian incident, I found the station filled with flood refugees, about four thousand of them, hungry, and often sick and dying. How pitifully they begged alms and food from those who got off the train. My heart was moved with compassion and I wanted to do something to help them—but what? To the question "Why, why are there such calamities?" my common sense told me that flood control measures could prevent such catastrophes but ignorance and lack of interest were responsible. Lyman Hoover, Y.M.C.A. secretary, and his wife met me and provided lodging for me. Mr. Hoover and I had worked together on the Student Volunteer Movement back in the States. They were very gracious hosts.

During my sojourn in that ancient city, Peiping, I experienced a dust storm for the first time. The whirling dust was so thick that it was scarcely possible to open one's eyes. I do not care to repeat such an experience. The modern city was built about the old Imperial City which was surrounded by walls twenty feet high. Here in the old palaces art, jewels and other treasures were displayed. One room contained clocks from all over the world. For centuries Peiping had been the cultural center of the Orient and I found unsurpassed embroideries, porcelains, cloisonne, Tibetan and Mongolian brass, carpets, rugs, silver and gold ornaments. On September 24 I visited the Temple of Heaven and suddenly realized that I was celebrating my birthday where the emperor used to offer prayer and sacrifices semiannually in the midst of great ceremony.

Here again I saw Chinese youth speaking on the streets against the Japanese disturbances in Manchuria. Everywhere were posters depicting masses of flood refugees as well as the Japanese rushing their army toward China and killing the people. The faces of some of the people thronging the streets were tense as they realized the true situation, while many others passed by unmoved by the oncoming threat. I had planned to take the Peiping-Mukden express to Manchuria in order to see the Great Wall of China and had already purchased my ticket when the Hoovers expressed grave concern about traveling that way because of the frequent sabotage of the railway. Accordingly I went to exchange my ticket to Mukden for one on another route. It was Saturday and I found that the agent was not at his office and so, given his home address, I took a ricksha to try to find him. Just as I rang the bell, he came out of the house with a tennis racket. How relieved he seemed when he saw me. He explained that he had been concerned about how he would find me to tell me that train service on that line had been suspended due to the prevailing tension. He advised me to take a train to Tientsin, and then a steamer to Dairen on the Manchurian border, then a South Manchurian train to Antung and from there to Pyongyang. I gladly followed his advice, and when the train crossed the railroad bridge from Antung I felt that I was truly at home again.

Sineuiju was the first station in Korea and here the late September air was crisp and invigorating, the sky a heavenly blue, and the fall foliage brilliant in color. I was in the same land with my children! I would soon see my mother and my mother-in-law. Korean women getting on the train with their familiar garb and hairdress and with babies on their backs caused a great wave of happiness to flow over me, followed by a great burden of regret because my fellow countrywomen were not free. Suddenly I felt again that I was hemmed in by circumstances. Five years and two months had passed since I left my homeland. I had seen much of the world, I had experienced freedom, moving freely among free peoples. Now I was coming back to my own people who were oppressed by the Japanese and also I must face my own personal problems which must be solved. I knew the action I was about to take in regard to my marital status would create a lot of criticism and I might have to pay for it all of my life. But unless ills were cured they would go on hurting. I would rather have an arm amputated and live than to die because it was diseased. I was confident that I would find a way to work out by own problem with God's help, but what of Korea's problems and the world's problems? I was certainly a part of the whole. Could I be used of God to help meet the larger problems also? Probably I was the first Korean woman in history to have a chance to know intellectual America as widely and intimately as had been my opportunity, and surely few Korean women had ever had an opportunity to encompass the globe with so many thoughtful friends in every country to interpret contemporary life. What could I now do with my understanding?

I I

The New Approach

When I arrived at Pyongyang station, my mother and a missionary friend, Grace Dillingham, were waiting to meet me. This was the second largest city in Korea and it was here that my mother and I had attended the Bible Institute together, and from here I had taken the train to Seoul as a little girl when I left for Ewha High School. Known for its lovely scenery, delicious water, beautiful women and delectable cold Korean noodles, Pyongyang had now become a great missionary center for the Presbyterians and Methodists, with hospitals, schools and colleges for both boys and girls. At that time there were many revolutionary political organizations working toward the overthrow of the Japanese regime. But all this was of secondary interest to me now, for within me was a burden heavier and more miserable than all the political and economic miseries surrounding me. Being bound by age-old concepts and traditions was the worst burden of all. I had learned that the most precious thing in the world is freedom to do what one believes is right and now I must choose between the Korean custom of remaining with my husband "no matter what," or starting out on an independent way of life.

As Mother and I met a long look of understanding passed

between us, and although no word was spoken, each knew what was in the mind of the other. When the opportunity to talk came, the first thing my mother said was, "Son, have you enough strength to overthrow the unfair weight which has piled up for many centuries upon our women?" My mouth felt so dry that I could not answer. After some little thought, she continued, "I know that you are very eager to see your little girls but before you see them I must tell you what has happened in your absence. Don't think that I want to interfere in your life, but today I am telling you this, not as your mother but as a woman who has suffered much, and also as a messenger from a just God. Your husband has a concubine. With what money? With the money you sent to care for your children. Whether the children got any of the money I do not know, but your mother-in-law has taken good care of them. Their father was off having a good time with his women at Buddhist temples and at summer resorts where they serve good food. Now I know what I think should be done and I believe you know, too. You should ask for a legal divorce. Your marriage was a mistake but there is no use continuing in a grave mistake. I just wonder whether you are strong enough to meet the criticism a divorce will bring."

This was a long speech for my mother; she usually spoke abruptly. Now we both fell silent, thinking of the same matters. A Korean woman never divorces her husband, although a Korean man may divorce his wife. Moreover, Christians did not approve of divorce. Nor, for that matter, did Mother and I approve of it except for the most serious of reasons. And we did not wish to do anything which reflected upon Christians. Furthermore, if my first move upon return to my homeland was to divorce my husband I would have no influence in educated circles; no prestige; indeed, probably no entrée. I would even seem to reflect discredit upon America.

Suddenly my mother went on. "All men are going to be very much afraid that you are establishing a precedent and that other women will follow it. You will be criticized for disturbing the peaceful trend of their lives. You will stand alone with only me to support you. If I were you I would not do anything hastily. But you face a decision."

We both sighed—but it was wonderful to have my mother to sigh with! Perhaps we were happier than if we had been joyful. From the station we went to Miss Dillingham's school, Chungeui Methodist Girls' School. There were about three hundred girls enrolled and one of them was Kim Kyong-Sook, the fourteen-year-old daughter of my high school classmate. I learned she had lost both parents not long ago and had five little brothers and sisters. When she discovered that I was her mother's close friend, she rushed to me and greeted me in tears as if her own mother had come to life again.

This contact left me thoughtful and serious. As I watched these young girls playing on the campus, my mind projected into their future. They were being educated to be more open-minded and practical than the women of the past for whom everything had been decided by the men. I, too, had had an education but I had allowed my emotions to overrun my judgment and had married a man from whom convention would not easily release me. I felt that it was right that I should be divorced from him, for I had learned the Christian way of life and I knew his way was wrong and that my influence would not make him change. I felt that I must decide to ask for a divorce for the sake of the future of all these girls. Nevertheless the decision seemed increasingly difficult for I had much to lose, most important the guardianship of my children, for Korean law gives children to the father. When I was divorced I would be all alone except for my mother—no husband, no children, no friends, no church.

Praying for divine guidance, I left Pyongyang the next day by plane for Seoul. My mother returned to her home in the village of Dukdong about forty miles to the southwest. Since this was my first plane trip I was practically glued to the windows but the nervous pacing of my one fellow traveler kept me in terror lest he upset the equilibrium of the plane. I sat with hands clenched so tightly that my palms were wet. The din of the motors was so loud that conversation was impossible. When the plane was flying over a city, the co-pilot handed me a message written in Chinese. It read, "We are passing by Kaesong and in fifteen minutes we will arrive in Seoul." In no time the plane flew over the mountains and I saw Seoul lying beneath us with the Han River threading its way through the harvested rice paddies. I recognized Namsan (South Mountain) where I had once contemplated taking my life.

It was wonderful to be met at the airport by a missionary friend and by Mrs. J. S. Ryang, an Ewha friend. She took me to her home and although she knew about the problems I was facing she did not mention them, waiting to see what my attitude would be. I had already made up my mind to take definite action. The sooner the better.

The next day, much to my surprise, a mutual friend of my husband's and mine came with a message from Woon-Ho, saying, "If you would like to have a divorce I will be very glad to give it to you for one thousand dollars plus our house." I had bought the house with my own earnings and had registered it in my mother's name. To my knowledge this was the first time in history that a Korean man had offered a divorce to his wife and had asked her for a financial settlement! My impulsive answer was "No, not on those terms!" The next day the friend returned and again urged me to accept the conditions and be done with the matter since we could never have a Christian home together and my husband might use my refusal to extort even more from me in the future. I thereupon accepted his demands in order to make an end to the intolerable situation.

With the decision made, the entire matter was soon settled. An old Korean proverb says, "A mountain of love cannot win a molehill of law." So now, although the law gave me my freedom, it gave the children to their father. My love had no persuasion before the law. However, I felt they would come to me eventually because they were girls and would want to come; also because my mother-in-law was in sympathy with me; and because their father would not have time or place for them if he should start a new home. But now I could not go to them. It would not be "the custom" and would cause hurt to my mother-in-law. The children would not suffer from waiting a while because they had care and affection where they were and I was really a stranger to them, no matter how much they had heard about me and treasured my picture. Mine was the heartache. For long months I had measured off the time against the day I should see them. And now time must again be measured off.

It is difficult for a Westerner to understand how my divorce, which seemed to me a "reasonable and moral right," affected my life. Because I had been divorced I could not get work. However, I was invited to live in the home of my Christian Korean friends, Dr. and Mrs. Hugh H. Cynn. But soon they also were shunned. I taught a Sunday School class which rapidly doubled in size but one Sunday we were asked to evacuate the room—because I had been divorced from a man with whom no Christian woman would live. I could no longer live a normal life.

My loyal Christian friends insisted on my remaining with them. The Cynns had both been educated in America and Dr. Cynn had traveled widely in America, Europe and the Orient, representing the Korean people in international church conferences. They had suffered much, losing three of their five children within a month from an epidemic. Only suffering could have made people understand as they did. They were undoubtedly the most intelligent, sympathetic and loving friends I had ever known. They advised me to forget myself in helping the women and children who so desperately needed help and their suggestion met a ready response in my heart.

The Cynns had a large living room. On the following Sunday afternoon I conducted a Sunday School class there with eight children who were playmates of the Cynn children. I told them stories, taught them songs, and we played games. My hosts supplied Korean candy and peanuts after the session. How we all enjoyed our first class! The next Sunday each child brought another one and our number was sixteen. On the third Sunday this number was doubled, and in a month we had no more room for the children. My friends' living-room walls were about to break out! There was no Christian church in our vicinity, so the news of our activity had been spreading in widening circles. Then the Cynns built a one-room building in their courtyard large enough to accommodate one hundred children. In this new place the children put on their own creative plays, invited their parents to attend, and the Cynn courtyard practically became a public playground.

After a time I began to attend the Sukkyo (Stone Bridge)

Methodist Church outside West Gate in Seoul. It was two miles over the hill. When I stood upon the hill where the old city wall used to be, I could get a good view of the city. Facing south I looked toward immovable, pine-covered, evergreen Namsan, symbol of the Korean people's spirit and patriotism; to the east there was the modern marble building of the Japanese Government from which the iron hand stretched forth to rule over my people; in the west stood the large West Gate Japanese jail where thousands of Koreans who had violated Japanese edicts had been imprisoned, and also the Sukkyo church, spiritual lighthouse for thousands of people in that area. I saw the need for help in this church and gave my services as choir leader. We even attempted to sing some Negro spirituals. At Christmas time we went into the slum area and sang carols and gave packages of rice, fresh meat and wood to the poor. One year we distributed packages to some fifty families.

My salvation lay in service. I became so involved with new undertakings that I had no time to worry about what people were saying about me. I organized a Business and Professional Women's Club in Seoul, the first of its kind. We had forty young women—teachers, nurses, doctors, shopkeepers, salesgirls, housewives, and the one and only taxi driver. This type of organization, cutting across class lines, was very important because the members gave encouragement and inspiration to one another.

As the club's first project we held the first Korean Women's Skating Contest in our history, using the Han River Rink which was used by the Men's Athletic Association. We had seventeen contestants although several of them could not skate five feet because skating for girls was a very new thing here. However, they were courageous enough to come out to the rink. To make it worse, I, the president of the club and boss of the show, could not even stand up on skates, so I wore a pair of straw shoes. We advertised the great event in all the leading papers and something like five thousand spectators—mostly men—came to view our efforts. Fortunately we had one expert woman skater and she gave us an exhibition of what it was possible for women and girls to accomplish in the way of skating. For days that skating exhibit was the talk of the city; indeed of the whole country. It had drawn a much larger crowd than had the events presented by the Men's Athletic Association.

Toward spring, after our success at presenting Korean sportswomen, I decided to instigate a few more modern innovations. Why not a fashion show? Certainly a fashion show should not arouse any antagonism. Our Business and Professional Women's Club simply buzzed with the idea. The drygoodsmen were appealed to successfully for donations; we obtained the use of the largest auditorium, that of the Y.M.C.A., on the main street; we drilled girls for the exhibit, arranged for homelike stage settings and obtained the services of a pianist. Then the women began to sew industriously. The idea behind this show was to make women and children's clothes more practical and attractive both in color and workmanship in order to bring out individual personality. We particularly wanted to stress the point that middle-aged and elderly ladies need not appear drab and colorless.

Again we publicized our efforts widely. The fashion show was held on a Saturday night with a correspondingly large crowd. In fact the hall was packed. Everything went along smoothly and our show was a huge success. The next day news comments were very gracious, stating that the "women who took part in the show looked very charming and graceful."

No adverse criticism was heard. The Business and Professional Women's Club had scored another hit.

However, my great desire was to work for the benefit of the women and children in the villages. If anyone needed guidance and help it was these people. Unless rural conditions could be improved they would continue to lead dwarfed existences. Three-quarters of the population were farmers, mostly tenants. The average size of the farms was four to five acres, one forty-eighth the size of the average American farm. Two-thirds of the land was owned by 2 per cent of the population, mostly Japanese. Tenants had to pay 40 to 50 per cent of their crops as rent. Most tenant farmers were never out of debt. They were literally diseased by poverty, a disease which could be cured only by the introduction of modern methods of agriculture, self-government, liberal education and the like. But under the Japanese there was no chance for such remedies. The purpose of the Japanese educational policy in Korea was to make Korean children loyal and dutiful subjects of Japan. At school in the "morals" hour, Japanese schoolteachers stressed emperor worship and the filial duty of a subject to a ruler, the old Confucian principle. All subjects were taught in the Japanese language.

Private and government schools for Korean children could only accommodate one out of four children, whereas the Japanese had well-equipped schools for all their own children. In the thirties the census showed that there were 70,000 students of high school level, about one-half Japanese although the resident Japanese were less than 3 per cent of the Korean population. There were 4,000 college students but the majority attended the Christian mission colleges. In the government Imperial University in Seoul, there were 350 Japanese students against 206 Koreans. What was the future of the Korean graduates of this university? If one got a teaching position he came home with a thin pay envelope, while his Japanese classmate who taught in the same school took home a fat one. Much credit should go to the Christian missionaries for Korea's modern education. But the Japanese put so many restrictions on these Christian schools as to what must be taught, how it must be taught, how many Japanese should be on the teaching staff, et cetera, that it became increasingly difficult to maintain a Christian school.

By far the worst lot fell to the village children. The majority could not go beyond the third grade due to their financial situation and so they stopped and worked on the farm to help their tenant fathers. Three out of every four school-age children remained entirely unlettered. Such a situation alarmed me. I therefore turned my footsteps in the direction of the villages.

In some of the villages surrounding Seoul I began night classes for women and children during the winter months. This was the best time to start, for the women were not busy in the fields and usually occupied themselves with weaving and sewing. I had one village each night, Monday through Friday, making the trips by train, trolley or walking. The care of babies and children was a starting point at each meeting, since child care was a subject close to every woman's heart. Picture cards depicting the various ways of handling babies in many other lands were passed about and discussed at great length. Other differences in child care were brought out and modern methods introduced. I always tried to point out how to improve their methods with what they had at hand and stressed gentleness and patience toward all.

For the children there were, of course, pictures and stories of children in other lands, and their ways of playing. The children caught onto games with such enthusiasm that other children were attracted to the classes. Later on we staged field days with the entire village participating in the games and contests, and many women happily admitted that they had not played or run since they were children, and they loved it. When it came to group singing the children joined in, but not the mothers or grandmothers. The reason was that only dancing girls learned to sing in order to entertain men in public, and it was heretofore considered immodest if any woman or girl did the same as the dancing girls. But soon these mothers were convinced that singing in itself was not wrong and great enjoyment was derived from the songs.

I also taught reading and writing, using the Korean phonetic alphabet. In the schoolroom the blackboard was used to good effect but in their homes the women had neither the equipment nor the time for practicing what they had learned. I suggested the use of the poker with which they stirred the fire while cooking, writing with it upon the earthen floor. This idea quickly spread and many women and children practiced writing in their homes without pencil or paper. Likewise in the fields at noontime they wrote with sticks upon the ground. The easier and more simple the tools, the better for all. Before long contests were held in reading and writing and such coveted prizes as paper and pencils, needles and thread, or soap and candy gave added incentive to these efforts.

Sanitation, which was so sorely needed, was introduced through the children. Prizes were offered to the children coming to school with the cleanest faces, hands and nails, and soon all of them ran to meet me to show me how worthy they were of the prize. This effort aroused in the mothers a consciousness of cleanliness which opened the way for the teaching of health and sanitation.

The village homes were mostly thatch-roofed cottages of two or three rooms, an attached kitchen and an outside toilet, the walls made of stones, mud and straw. Windows and doors were lattice covered with paper. And as a rule the inside walls of rooms were also papered. Kerosene lamps or candles were used for lighting purposes. There were better homes, of course, which were thatch-roofed with stone walls part way to the roof. The few really fine homes had tiled roofs and stone walls, more rooms and an inner court as well as an outer court. Always the elaborate home had a private well, but the rest of the village was served by a few public wells.

Although barley, millet, soybeans, sorghum and corn were raised, each woman yearned for a good rice field for Korean rice is highly prized and regulates the prices of other commodities. The village women wanted to own good homes and also to earn some cash. Through the consumer's co-operative method which I had observed in Denmark, commodities were purchased wholesale by a common fund established by the contributions of each member of the group. Then these commodities, such as soap, kerosene, cooking oil, et cetera, were sold at retail over a period of three months and the profits were divided among the original contributors. The capital was reinvested and the same procedure repeated. This method saved both the time involved in shopping and the amount of money which would otherwise have gone to the middleman. The movement started first in about a dozen villages but spread far beyond.

"Doing once is worth learning ten times" was proved over and over again in these co-operative activities. Husbands and sons respected their women when they had some earning power. For example, a middle-aged woman who was a member of the first co-operative society met me after the first three-month period and with face shining told me of her own wonderful experience. She said, "Teacher, you don't know what you have done for me. My husband drinks; we are tenant farmers and very poor; and he has always poured out all of his grievances upon me and our three girls. One night he mistreated me and told me to leave our home and to take the girls with me. He said that the girls and I were only liabilities. Then I replied, 'Very well, I will go but how can you make a living without me?' and opening my purse I showed him the brand new five-yen bill I had earned through the co-operative. I told him that I had learned the secret of making money and after he thought for a while he said to me, 'I've changed my mind. Don't go.' Teacher, my husband now respects me."

For four years I continued this work with money given by individuals in America and sent through Miss Woodford, general secretary of the Florida Chain of Missionary Assemblies who had promised to be responsible for this fund. Had it not been for this assistance our work could not have prospered and spread. We soon left the original classes to local leadership and added new villages to our route with the aim of showing more people a new way of life and a new hope in the light of Jesus Christ.

During these busy years I became aware of two great needs: first, an organization of those who were interested in rural work, and second, a leadership training center for village women and children in order to develop leaders. Accordingly I organized the Society for Rural Women and Children with one hundred and fifty members. The training center depended on the success of the organization for rural work and had to be shelved to await developments.

Aside from my rural work I wrote three books in Korean, *Danish Folk High Schools, Pointers for Rural Workers,* and *My World Travels.* I also translated into Korean *From Jerusalem to Jerusalem* by Helen Barrett Montgomery, and a book for little children, *Little Lord Jesus* by Lucy W. Peabody. Mrs. Montgomery and Mrs. Peabody donated the funds for the publication of their books. These were very critical days in my personal life and the responsibility and pressure of activity helped stabilize my whole future.

I also built a home of my own design near Sajik Park. The lot which I had purchased used to be a part of the Dojung Palace which was then 450 years old. In our country, homes have always been built with little thought for the convenience of the housewife who spends much of her time in the kitchen. The homes were built on more than one level with the kitchen on the earth level and the rest of the house elevated. Shoes were worn in the kitchen but not in the living quarters so they had to be removed when going from the kitchen to the other parts of the house. In North Korea a door connected the kitchen with the living quarters but in South Korea there was no door between; consequently it was necessary to carry the cooked food from kitchen to the outdoors and then into the living quarters, thereby chilling the food as well as the cook in cold weather. Living quarters were used as bedroom, living room and dining room. Bedding was rolled up in the morning and the bedroom became a dining room where breakfast and other meals were served. After the meal the trays of food and dishes were taken outside and back to the kitchen and the room was used for living, sewing and other family activities.

With all of these inconveniences in mind, particularly with regard to a kitchen, I planned my house carefully. It had central living quarters with a bedroom on either side, with a kitchen and bathroom opening from this common living room by sliding doors. The kitchen had running water and work counters where the food could be prepared while standing rather than the cook's having to squat to work on the floor or low stand; the sink had a tin lining and good sewage outlet, and the bathroom had a wash bowl and a Japanese tub with a firebox underneath.

When my house was finished Mother came to live with me. After all these years! When I invited her to share my home she said, "I will not come unless I'm needed. I have my own home, my flowers, my friends and my church, and I am able to care for myself. But if you need me, I'll be glad to come." All of her life she had shown this independent spirit. She made one other provision, also, which was so much like her. She said, "I must have my dogs with me." It was the same situation as when she was married. I was very glad to have her, dogs and all.

Mother disposed of her house and lot, which she had paid for by her own earnings from weaving and peddling, by making a present of it to her church at Dukdong. It was a simple, thatch-roofed house surrounded by a profusion of flowers from early spring until late fall. On Sunday mornings a Sunday School class held its sessions there and when anyone remarked on how spick and span everything was she would say, "A Christian home should be clean and sparkling. If our homes are not different from those of non-Christians, what have we learned from our new religion?" She bought a portable reed organ and gave it to the grammar school which was conducted by her church, and the kindergarten was the proud recipient of a clock. She had three sets of pulpit chairs made and these were given to the three churches in her district. Her dishes and furniture went to my uncle and his wife.

When Mother came to me she brought her Bible, a bolt of cloth of her own weaving, a few clothes, her dogs, some Korean black taffy, and matches. The matches signified the hope for the rapid spreading of wealth, like fire, for the family newly moved into a home. Taffy stretches, and so it symbolized expanding wealth and household. She also brought two hammered brass bowls, one for rice and one for water. These lovely bowls were her personal gifts to me. They were over a hundred years old and they vibrated with a beautiful resonance when struck. The water bowl had a two-tone vibration and would reverberate for nearly two minutes.

As if having my mother with me were not joy enough, my girls, Iris and Lotus, were suddenly free to join us. Their father had remarried and did not wish to have responsibility for them, and so with their paternal grandmother's loving permission they came to my mother and me. They were excited to come and I was almost tongue-tied with emotion. But all of us were shy. We felt closer through our letters than face to face. The first few hours we were very polite. And then all at once we were a family. Our tongues loosed. The girls were not as old-fashioned as I feared they might be and I was not as modern as they feared I might be. In a sense my mother was the interpreter of our spirits until we got going together.

The two girls were different in many ways, as sisters are likely to be. Lotus was twelve years old. Born under the sign of the monkey she was witty and intelligent; although she was no chatterer, when she made a comment it was usually clever. She had a way of turning words and of settling a matter with a cryptic remark. She was musical, playing the piano and singing alto. As time went on she also developed marked gifts in dramatics. In looks she resembled my mother and she had her good health. Her other grandmother had seen to it that she was a good cook. I always had a special pride in watching Lotus.

But then I would turn and have a special pride in Iris. Being two years older she was less reticent in speaking her opinion. In disposition she was highly optimistic and could usually figure a way out of a predicament. Still she had a spirit of reserve so that strangers rather hesitated to make advances. It was a dignity which became her. I delighted in her black wavy hair and her fair complexion with rosy cheeks. One eyelid is oriental with no fold on the lid but the other has a fold. Through her early years she had been a delicate child and was always given the preference in food. But in our own home all shared equally and her grandmother's good cooking pleased us all. Iris also loved music. The world might be in turmoil but at home we had many happy serene hours. I never get enough of looking back on them.

During those years, 1931 to 1935, when I was devoting my time to church and rural work, the Japanese Government was concentrating on prepartion for further invasions, demanding from us more labor, more agricultural and industrial products. After they seized Mukden they set up a puppet state in Manchuria with Henry Pu Yi, the last of China's Manchu dynasty, as ruler. The puppet state was called Manchukuo—country of the Manchus. After they succeeded in their Manchurian invasion the Japanese visibly became more confident and arrogant. From that time on their policy was to march into China and beyond, accompanied by the rattling of swords. In 1932 they invaded Shanghai; in 1935, North China. China surrendered rule over Peiping and Tientsin. It was only a series of steps then into Mongolia, China proper, and finally Pearl Harbor. In the meantime Japan had two European sympathizers—Germany and Italy. In the Korean newspapers, which were censored by the Japanese, accounts of the daring actions of Hitler and Mussolini were constantly heralded. Germany became increasingly turbulent and truculent, reported to us as courageous and determined. In 1933 Hitler was made absolute dictator with complete control of all activities—political, economical, industrial, commercial and cultural. He repudiated the Treaty of Versailles, ignored the League of Nations, re-established universal military training, demanded union with Austria and part of Czechoslovakia. He also developed air and navy prowess. He started persecuting the Jews. Under his tutelage the Saar territory taken from Germany by the Treaty of Versailles voted for reunion with Germany. In January, 1935, Mussolini mobilized 70,000 troops and began to invade Ethiopia, completed the invasion the next year, and annexed that country. Emperor Haile Selassie and his family fled from Addis Ababa and King Victor Emmanuel of Italy was made Emperor of Ethiopia. In November, 1936, Germany and Japan signed an Anti-Comintern pact. A year later, Italy joined them in the same treaty and quit the League of Nations. Thus was formed the Rome-Berlin-Tokyo Axis, a newly united force to invade and to attack more peoples and countries.

Although most thoughtful Koreans made few comments aloud, they sensed that another world war was coming. My mother and I used to talk about it. Before it came I wanted to make another trip to America. We needed help for our rural work. Also I felt a kind of desperation in wanting Americans to understand what was going on. If they could feel the strangling of Korea they might prevent disaster for themselves. Many American missionaries had come to my country. Now I felt driven to be a kind of missionary to America. Americans must understand that all they had said about the brotherhood of mankind was true, and that one nation could not suffer slow extinction without endangering other nations. Would I have time to make a trip to America and return before the catastrophe? I thought so. Indeed, the time seemed propitious, for the girls were happily settled into their routines, Lotus in the Government High School for Girls and Iris at Ewha High, my alma mater. Mother would look after them. She was never reluctant to carry responsibility, and especially for my sake. In her eyes there was nothing her son-daughter could not accomplish. While walking to my village classes on many lonely trips, I talked the matter over with God. Jesus had said, "And all things, whatsoever ye shall ask in prayer, believing, ye shall receive." I believed I should again go to America.

12

Taking Korea to America

One day two letters came in the same mail, one from the general secretary of the Student Volunteer Movement, Jesse R. Wilson, asking me to speak at their Quadrennial Convention on New Year's Day, 1936, in Indianapolis; the other from B. Louise Woodford, inviting me to speak at the 1936 Chain of Missionary Assemblies held in Florida. These letters seemed an answer to my prayer for guidance. However, pleased as I was at these invitations, I realized how difficult it would be to get a passport to return to America, but felt deep in my heart that the passport would be forthcoming because the invitations were unsolicited and there must have been a reason for them. After applying for my passport and waiting a reasonable length of time, I went to the Japanese officials to inquire why it had not been granted. Excuses were given for days, until I finally decided to do something definite about the matter. I went to the officer in charge and told him that if the passport were not granted to me, the two organizations in America inviting me to speak would certainly consider my not being allowed to leave Korea very strange. After weighing this point of view carefully, he finally gave his consent. Such an experience taught me that it was always best to deal directly with those in authority.

Again it rained on the November day I left the Seoul station. This time it was a pleasant trip in prospect because I was returning to a familiar country. From Pusan I took a ship to Shimonoseki, then a train to Tokyo where I was a guest of. Florence Cynn Chang and her husband who was a student there. They were very gracious hosts and the proud parents of two adorable children. I am afraid I talked about my children also. My week with them went all too quickly and before I knew it they were accompanying me to Yokohama where I embarked.

On this trip I took a Japanese freighter, the *Kano Maru,* which was sailing to America via the Panama Canal for a load of scrap iron. In those days America had no qualm about selling scrap iron to Japan. There were twelve passengers aboard and I shared a stateroom with Edith Sato of Philadelphia whose parents, a Japanese father and a German-American mother, were on board also. Among the passengers was a Japanese businessman who was making his fortieth Pacific crossing. If this one man could cross the Pacific forty times, why were we Koreans hemmed in? Why could we not also have business connections across the seas?

Our first stop was San Pedro, California, thence along the coast past Mexico and into the Panama Canal at Balboa. The passage of the ship through the three locks took us eighty-five feet above sea level and back to sea level again in the course of fifty miles. Fascinated by this climbing of hills in boats via water ladders, I recalled the motto of the canal builders—"We are here to do the impossible." My feeling with regard to Korea and my people was much the same. That day I counted the flags of thirteen different nations. One ship was a Russian whale boat with sturdy women for a crew. I hoped it would not be many years before Korean boats passed through this canal.

After a short stop at Cristobal on the Atlantic side of the Canal, we sailed up the coast directly to New York. On the morning of Friday, December 13 (my lucky thirteen again), Lillian Nilson from the Student Volunteer Movement brought me a batch of mail, "welcome home" letters sent by numerous friends and acquaintances. I was most grateful to be made welcome in America. As soon as the news of my return to the States got around, invitations began to pour in. The first one came from Mrs. Robert M. Russell, of Larchmont, New York, whose husband was minister of the Larchmont Presbyterian Church which had previously given me donations for my rural work. It was a very happy experience to pick up threads of acquaintanceship and carry on once more.

Along came the Christmas holidays which I spent in Ridgewood, New Jersey, at the home of Mr. and Mrs. W. A. Hardenbergh whom I had known since my Columbia University days. Their daughters, Margaret and Kathryn, were much the same age as my girls, which fact in itself cemented our relationship. For many years while I traveled about the United States these good friends urged me to make their home my headquarters and I feel eternally grateful to them for their generosity. The Christmas decorations that year made a different impression on me than heretofore for many trees were lighted with brilliant blue bulbs which indicated that Oriental tones were becoming popular. To our minds the silvery blue-gray colors denote mystic qualities. The singing of Christmas carols, the laughter of children, the joy of giving appeared to overflow everywhere. Everyone radiated happiness. What a different situation this was from the one I so recently left.

The day after Christmas I left for Indianapolis to attend the Student Volunteer Quadrennial Convention for which I had come to America. Among other speakers from the Orient were Toyohiko Kagawa of Japan and T. Z. Koo of China. Representatives and delegates from Canada and the United States as well as a number of overseas students, totaling three thousand in all, assembled in one place with one goal—to evangelize the world. It was a moving experience to see these young people planning courageously to achieve their objectives. I had spoken at the Detroit Quadrennial Convention on New Year's Day eight years previously and my speech had taken eleven minutes. Now my talk extended to thirty minutes.

My next assignment was with the Florida Chain of Missionary Assemblies, beginning in January, 1936. Frank Laubach and Muriel Lester were speakers on the Chain that year. In four weeks I spoke ninety-seven times from Jacksonville to Miami, filling in often for other speakers. After the Florida tour was over, I went to Canada where the Canadian Student Christian Movement and the United Church of Canada sponsored a six-week speaking tour. I spoke in every province from Halifax to Victoria. The Canadian people and students were reserved and conservative, courteous and dependable. I was always perturbed at how little Korea was known to the world in general. There were very few Korean students in Canada, practically no books on Korea, and consequently nobody knew about Korea except through missionary channels. In a way I felt that the Japanese had succeeded in hiding Korea away from the eyes of the world. She was their own little oyster.

As I traveled from the east coast to the west coast of Canada the immensity of the country surprised me. It was indeed a vast land with its forests, farms, mines, fisheries, Rockies, prairies, lakes and—its most precious gem—Lake Louise.

Among the outstanding experiences I had on my Canadian tour one lingers in my mind. From Digby to Halifax a retired president of The Bank of Nova Scotia drove me in his car, keeping up a running conversation as he told me bits of the history of Canada, about the problems she faced and of her place in world affairs. Before reaching Halifax we came to a long, absolutely straight stretch of road with a house sitting directly in the middle, as though the road went through the center of the house. He told me about a grandmother and child who were driving along this same stretch of road; when the child was afraid they would have to drive directly through the house the grandmother reassured her that when they reached that point they would find that the road circled the house. He concluded, "And so it is with life. Never worry when some obstacle seems to lie ahead. The solution will be there when you get to it." I've always remembered this old banker and his philosophy. He rather reminded me of my mother's turn of mind.

I traveled in the States the remainder of the trip, speaking in colleges and universities, high schools, churches, men's civic organizations and women's clubs. In twenty months I made 642 speeches and covered 80,000 miles. The subject of all of my addresses was the deplorable condition of farmers and their families in Korea. Then I described the efforts we had put forth the past four years. I explained how I had learned that one of the best ways to help raise spiritual and economic standards was first to provide help in a physical way. Since our farms were small, tractors were not practical but oxen or cows were needed to plow and to use as beasts of burden.

Every farmer hoped to own a cow but not many could afford a whole cow. And so for centuries Korean farmers have been raising and owning cows co-operatively. Sometimes three families own a cow, or each owns one-third of a cow, and the owners take turns using the cow, being responsible for its well-being. The calves are also raised co-operatively and when one is old enough to do one-half of a day's work, the mother cow is sold and the profit divided among the owners. Not only in their cow plan but in their workaday program, farmers have labored co-operatively for centuries, hoeing, harvesting and threshing by hand. Each farmer loans his farm-hand to a neighbor at a needy period and in turn he receives help in like manner. Thus the co-operative community spirit is developed. My idea was to get some co-operative cows for the villages where our rural work had been started. If I could get enough money for fifty co-operative cows, nearly one hundred and fifty families would be benefited. If I could encourage a Sunday School class, a college, a women's club or a church women's society in America to adopt a co-operative project for a special village, I would be accomplishing something constructive for my people. I usually ended my talks by saying that one co-operative cow on a Korean farm could do far more effective work than a thousand words.

On this trip I secured money from friends to purchase several co-operative cows. In those days in Korea a young, lean cow cost about thirty dollars, and when she was fattened up, the owners made a good profit. Cows were often given names by these generous friends, such as "Carillon" purchased by the Lake Wales (Florida) Methodist Church and Sunday School. Since this was a difficult word for Korean tongues to pronounce, we ended by calling her "Singing Cow." In Northfield, Massachusetts, the people contributed money for a cow and called her "Betsy Moo" after Betsy (Mrs. Dwight L.) Moody. The Kappa Phi girls of Miami University of Oxford, Ohio, called their cow "Ox-Ford." (They also made me an honorary member of their sorority at that time.) Donations were received in Canada also, and all together a total of thirty-three cows would be purchased for Korean villages. At about the same time Mrs. R. L. Fox of Leesburg, Florida, gave seven hundred dollars in memory of her late husband. Her sister, too, gave one hundred dollars. These gifts were used to start the proposed Training Center for Rural Leaders in Korea. Others donated from five dollars upward to help with this new undertaking.

During the summer of 1936 while I was speaking at different conferences, the eleventh Olympics was held in Berlin. A young Korean, Kitei Son (whose Korean name was Son Kee-Jung), went on the Japanese team and won the Marathon race of 26 miles, 385 yards, in 2 hours, 29 minutes and 19.2 seconds, setting the fastest record in the history of the Olympic Marathon race up to that date. We Koreans were happy over it beyond description but he was reported in the world press as a Japanese. However, in the Korean newspapers editorials were devoted to his marvelous achievement as a Korean and the consequences were very unhappy. The papers were suspended indefinitely and the editors spent many months in the Japanese jail. On the other hand the young man's victory aroused the ambition of other Korean youths and as a result, in 1947, eleven years after his victory and two years after Korea's liberation, a few young Koreans went to Boston to run the Unicorn Marathon under the Boston Athletic Association. Suh Yun-Bok won the race. Then the next year when the first postwar Olympics opened in Wembley, England, a Korean team entered and scored fifteen points. Two years later, in 1950, shortly before the North Korean Communist invasion of South Korea, three young men went to Boston and ran in the Unicorn Marathon again. This time they came in first, second and third, wearing the emblem of the Korean flag on their jerseys. They were cheered by a throng of spectators numbering five hundred thousand.

During my speaking trip I was concerned over the dropping off of church attendance. I spoke for churches more than for any other organization but only the rear seats were taken, no matter how large the church. Often I had the impression that the entire church might tilt backwards.

Of still further concern was the lack of knowledge of the Far Eastern situation, particularly in regard to the Japanese. Since the Russo-Japanese War, Japan had been prospering and maintained a strong army and a splendid navy. She also had modern educational facilities and many industries for her rapidly increasing population. She needed more room for expansion and there were the vast areas of China, French Indo-China, Burma, Malaya, Java, Sumatra and hundreds of islands of the North and South and Central Pacific at hand, mostly in the control of European powers. After World War I, Japan had been awarded mandate over the islands in the Western Pacific formerly held by Germany. She claimed them as her permanent possessions. She also established settlements in some Latin-American countries by arrangement with those countries. Those who knew Japan watched with anxiety when the United States wanted the island of Yap, one of the Carolines under Japanese mandate, to be internationalized so that the American cable to the Orient could have a relay station there. We also saw the mounting anti-Japanese feeling in the State of California and feared the consequences of the Japanese Exclusion Act. When we Koreans put all of these jigsaw puzzle pieces together, we could picture clearly what might come about between America and Japan. Yet the American people were either not informed or not convinced of the real situation and consequently were horrified by what later took place.

It was the summer of 1937 that I worried the most about impending events. I was attending the Fourth Pan-Pacific Women's Conference in Vancouver on July 7, when Japan landed her army in China. No woman had come from Korea to attend this important meeting because such representation had to be arranged through Japanese sanction, and so I had been invited by my Canadian friends to be one of four guest speakers. There were representatives from the Philippines, China and Japan, although China and Japan were now definitely hostile. I was especially interested in the attitudes of their delegates when the news of the Japanese invasion of China was flashed to us; they happened to be standing together and both seemed perfectly calm but the Japanese representative showed signs of regret. Women of various professions—teachers, nurses, doctors, lawyers, artists, business women—held discussions on methods of promoting peace in the Pacific. One of the unforgettable events was the visit of the entire delegation to the Peace Gate between the State of Washington, U.S.A., and British Columbia, with its inscribed vow of lasting peace between the two nations. The summer day was golden and a large shepherd dog was resting directly under the arch, and I wondered why all mankind did not form some sort of an alliance and peacefully rest as this dog was doing.

Not knowing how far the war might spread or how long it might last, I felt a great urge to hurry home to my daughters and my mother, and to my country, and so on August 14, 1937, I sailed from New York on the Italian liner, *S.S. Vulcania*. On this trip I felt much more secure in my personal affairs than formerly; secure, too, in the knowledge that many friends were backing me in my new work. My greatest concern was the pending war in the East.

Our first port of call was the Azores. A Czechoslovakian girl, Marta Soltesz, returning to her homeland, joined a French woman and me for a trip ashore. My most vivid memory of the Azores is the agony of the French woman in her fantastically high heels. Next we stopped at Lisbon and the chief picture which remains in my mind is of a young mother selling handmade baskets with her twin babies lying on the ground beside her. We sailed around the Spanish coast to Gibraltar. Spain was then a battleground not only of weapons but of clashing ideas, with the Civil War being fought out between the Nationalists, led by General Franco, and the loyalists. There were memorable moments. When our steamer arrived in Gibraltar I met the Prudential Life Insurance trade mark face to face. On a summer evening as we passed through the strait between Africa and Europe a heavenly cool breeze stirred the Mediterranean. In Algiers the French lady with the high heels disembarked for good while Miss Soltesz and I wandered among the Moslem mosques. In Algiers the French were of course in power. Recalling the activities of Hitler and Mussolini, I felt rather uncomfortable for the French people. After Algiers we stopped in Palermo and Naples where Miss Soltesz took a train to Czechoslovakia and I transferred to the Japanese steamer, *Terukuni Maru,* and headed toward home. (Thirteen months after I parted from my Czech friend, the Munich Conference dismembered Czechoslovakia. Ten years later I met Miss

Soltesz at the Mt. Lebanon Methodist Church in Pittsburgh. What a happy reunion that was and what a lot we had to tell each other.)

We traveled through the Suez Canal to Colombo, the home of Ceylon tea. I went up to Kandy, old capital of Ceylon, where the Temple of the Sacred Tooth honors the burial place of one of Buddha's teeth. The guide told me that many hundreds of years ago several young Koreans had made the trip all the way from Korea to these temples to study Buddhism, walking most of the distance, and that some of them had died and were buried in Kandy. In Colombo I was surprised to see a great deal of merchandise marked "made in Japan," and the Indian salespeople, thinking I was Japanese, spoke to me in that language. In Singapore I also found that great changes had taken place in the six years since my last visit. The Japanese were everywhere, the big stores well filled with their goods and the native salespeople speaking Japanese with pride. I saw all too clearly that the Japanese were preparing to take over what the British and the Dutch still dominated in Southeast Asia.

Arriving in Hong Kong, we heard that Japanese soldiers were fighting the Chinese near Canton, including air raids in their tactics. Although we had been scheduled to stop in Shanghai, the call was canceled and the ship went directly to Kobe. Here the hustle and bustle of war was evident. I took a train to Shimonoseki, then a steamer to Pusan where much to my surprise and delight my faithful friend, Mrs. Hugh H. Cynn, and her son met me. We traveled together to Seoul. After only twenty-two months' absence my country was so changed that I could scarcely believe my eyes. Japanese soldiers were everywhere, Japanese people stood about in the station waving Japanese flags, and my beloved Korea seemed to be submerged completely. I knew that war years were ahead of us and I was deeply grateful to be home where I could look after my family and perhaps even help my own country.

13

War Years

The most startling thing about the Korea to which I came back in September, 1937, was that I could not understand what the people, including my own daughters, were saying; nor could I make myself understood as everybody was speaking Japanese. Koreans no longer felt comfortable speaking their own language. Not being allowed to use Korean and not knowing Japanese, I was certainly in difficult circumstances. During my absence my girls had used Japanese, which they had previously been taught in school, so constantly that their Korean was no longer fluent enough for intimate conversation. The first time I went to the post office to ask for stamps in Korean, I was ignored, the clerks pretending that they did not know what I was saying. Stores, restaurants, schools and even homes had adopted the Japanese language completely. I was deeply pained at the implication. I wondered how the common people could have learned the language so quickly and soon discovered that those who could not speak Japanese were not speaking where they could be heard. Determined to be able to talk with my girls and to adjust myself to this new situation, I decided to study Japanese. If others could learn it, I could too. In the meantime, however, I urged Iris and Lotus to talk to me in Korean in the privacy of our own home, but Iris said, "Mother, you just don't understand! You have been away for almost two years and during that time something has happened that is too big for us."

And so I purchased a Japanese reader and began to learn the Japanese phonetic alphabet. One day the daughter of one of my former college friends came to call, and in the course of conversation she said that she did not think her mother understood her any more, that she felt her mother was too conservative. This remark made me realize that my daughters might feel the same way about me and I resolved to keep up with Korea's brand of the modern trend. My girls were reading magazines written in Japanese, so I too would read them. We have a saying, "If one wants to catch a tiger one must get to the place where tigers are."

I soon resumed teaching the Bible class for college men and women in our church, starting with one young man, my minister's son, who was attending Chosen Christian College. Within four weeks the class numbered thirty-two. We had wonderful discussions of the various world religions in the light of Christianity but soon I had to give up, due to Japanese pressure. We were not allowed to group a number of young people together under the sanction of a church for fear things other than religion might be discussed. Also the Japanese language was not being used in the class so that we were violating another of the national pressures. I was not yet ready to teach in Japanese.

However, my rural work continued. Within two years, with the gifts given by my American friends, largely Mrs. R. L. Fox of Leesburg, Florida, I built two cottages in the village of Yangcoke (which means Sunnydale). Here I conducted classes for women from the surrounding villages, using the larger cottage for classes and the smaller one for housing teachers. In the summer the cottages were used as a day nursery while the mothers worked in the fields, grandmothers and little sisters caring for the babies. During the winter months classes were held for mothers and co-operative buying was again begun.

During the time I was involved in this project, World War II broke out in Europe, and the Japanese War in China was becoming more intense. While my day-by-day work went on routinely, the German armies won in Poland, invaded Denmark and Norway, The Netherlands, Belgium and Luxemburg. The French Maginot Line crumbled; the German Air Force (*Luftwaffe*) rained bombs on England. France fell. Although Germany and Russia had signed a ten-year pact on September 27, 1939, for the fourth partition of Poland, Hitler ordered his armies into Russia on June 22, 1941. The Germans swept across the Ukraine and on to Leningrad, threatening Moscow. Hitler's war machine rolled through the Balkans and across to the rim of North Africa toward the Suez Canal, threatening the British life line. It was indeed *blitzkrieg* warfare. Hitler's spectacular campaigns were reported in the Japanese newspapers with praise and admiration for his skill and daring.

At the same time, in China, Generalissimo Chiang Kaishek and his Nationalist Army resisted the Japanese as valiantly as they could. The Korean Provisional Government, organized in Shanghai during the Independence Movement of 1919, had a Korean Army fighting with the Chinese against Japan.

Syngman Rhee was named first president of this Korean Government-in-exile.

Japan began to deport American missionaries and others whom she considered undesirable, and leading Koreans suspected of sympathy for America were put into jail. In place of Christianity the Japanese tried to substitute Shintoism, the worship of the emperor, whom they considered a man-god with divine lineage. They insisted that we Koreans and Japanese were all of one race and came from the same ancestry so that we should unite for greater power, and work together for the prosperity of all Asia and all Asians. Up to this time we Koreans had been treated as a second-rate people. Now, suddenly, tactics were reversed. We were promoted to the level of the Japanese and forced to adopt Japanese names. We Koreans have a saying, "Only dogs would change their names," but those who did not do so were treated as dogs. Children who did not change their names could not enter school. In many cases fathers had to change for the sake of their children's welfare.

School children and adults were then forced to bow at the Shinto shrines. The mission schools protested when the Japanese demanded that they too join these practices, but those schools which would not co-operate had various privileges taken away. Many Christian ministers and teachers were imprisoned and persecuted because they would not bow. Others thought it wiser to go through the form of obedience and therefore went to the shrines and bowed down before them while praying in their hearts to their Christian God.

At this stage my work in Yangcoke was becoming constantly more difficult because of lack of transportation. Each time I went there I took a bus. Since gasoline was at a premium, buses and other motors were run by charcoal-burning engines. My trip of thirty miles from Seoul was made by a bus with a grumbling, coughing, sputtering engine and we passengers frequently had to get off and push. Instead of the bus carrying us, we carried it. It was not fun on the bitter cold days. One day when I reached Yangcoke the village authorities advised me to close up my work. Since the Japanese were holding the handle of the knife and I had the blade, I decided I had better find another way of working for my people.

So I sold my two cottages and with the funds built a school on an empty lot which I owned in Seoul. The school seated sixty with chairs and one hundred without, and it had the basement four feet above the ground. I obtained a permit to teach girls who had graduated from high school, giving them an intensive, thorough one-year course in homemaking. These girls were mostly too young to be married immediately after graduation or lacked family funds to go to college. But one year of training was highly useful to them. I called the school Dukwha Institute, "duk" meaning "virtue" and "wha" meaning "peace." Parents were delighted with the school, for while their daughters received training in homemaking they were also being trained in leadership. Also while their daughters studied, parents could be looking for suitable husbands. I finally had an enrollment of thirty day students with one fulltime teacher and three parttime teachers. A well-supervised home near by was provided for those who lived too far to travel back and forth each night and morning.

This undertaking was a real success, as proved by the fact that the girls trained in this school married quickly. The second year the school was even better attended as the news spread that the girls from Dukwha Institute made particularly good wives and daughters-in-law. This effort represented in a small way what I wanted to do for all Korean women. In the past girls used to learn cooking, sewing and certain proprieties required of daughters-in-law and wives according to the old traditional ways, and then married the men whom their families had chosen for them. But in Dukwha we gave a new perspective and presented definite responsibilities to these prospective wives and future mothers, teaching them how to conform to the old customs and yet to be resilient, resourceful individuals.

On December 8, 1941 (Korean time), one of the teachers came into my office and broke the news of the Pearl Harbor attack. Japan had bombed and badly crippled the great American naval base in the Pacific. On the same day Japan bombed the Philippines. From that time on, like her Axis-friend, Germany, she had victory after victory. She invaded Malaya and sank British battleships off that coast. She seized Thailand, Guam, Midway and Wake. Hong Kong fell. She invaded Burma, Sumatra and Java. Singapore fell. She landed on New Guinea. Bataan and Corregidor surrendered also. She landed on Attu in the Aleutians. In Korea the Japanese people practically walked on air. All schools were ordered to send students to parade to the Namsan Shinto Shrine to celebrate the successive falls of Hong Kong, Singapore and the rest. As the war went on and Japan set up puppet governments in "occupied China," the Philippines, Burma and Indo-China she had very little co-operation from the native peoples. This was a thing we Koreans sensed in spite of Japanese reports to the contrary.

In Korea mass regimentation began. Most important was the People's Mobilization League under whose direction precincts were organized, made up of some fifteen families. Japanese undercover workers kept track of each family, visitors, why they came, when and where they went. It seemed as if the Japanese almost knew what each individual thought. If a certain number of men and women were needed for any purpose the neighborhood group supplied them. When metal was needed to make weapons, the people were forced to donate their brass bowls, spoons and utensils. I knew many families had buried their brass heirlooms in the earth in order to keep them. If the designated number of people or things were not forthcoming, woe to the neighborhood group leader! Students were drafted to work in the fields, to build roads and an airport. They were also given premilitary training, very strict and rigid. Then they were forced to volunteer as student soldiers. Even though most of these boys did not want to serve as soldiers they were caught in a net from which they could not escape. The authorities claimed that the Koreans were given the "honor and privilege" of dying for the emperor.

In the villages where my work had been established each farmer was given a quota for his crops and if he did not meet this quota he was punished beyond description. I knew farmers who were beaten all night long by their Japanese masters for not meeting the quota. Of course such treatment was short-sighted for the injured farmer could not produce. Besides growing food and cotton every person from seven to seventy-five throughout the rural areas was required to go into the hills to cut branches and dig roots of pine trees from which the pitch would be extracted to make turpentine. Thus farmers worked from dawn to dusk in their fields and then on to midnight in the hills. In return they had nothing but fear and hunger.

In December, 1944, the third year of Dukwha Institute's

existence, the ever-tightening web of Japanese intrigue and pressure became so strong that my school was forced to close, along with many others. We felt that we had been purged, emptied, made useless. I had put everything I had into the school—money, energy, time; in fact I had lived for this work. When the school closed I lost my best weapon in behalf of my people.

All this time Mother had been keeping house for us while Iris and I worked in Dukwha and Lotus was studying in Ewha College. After Iris finished Ewha she taught music in my school. The closing of the school was a sad blow to all of us. But Mother, with her great faith and insight, said to me, "I do not know what all these things mean but I do know that the Japanese are wrong for they had no right to come into our country and run it. This tyranny has to stop and somehow I believe that this war will give us our freedom." And so she encouraged us, assuring us that the suffering we were enduring was like birth pangs and that the Allied Forces were like the midwives who would deliver us. To me she said, "This door is closed but another door will open for you." She did not want me to lose heart entirely. Actually experience had taught both of us that God always opened other and greater doors when one was shut against us.

A few months after Dukwha was closed, my next-door neighbor hurried into our house saying breathlessly, "Come out quickly, three B-29's are flying so high over Seoul that they look like doves, with smoke trailing across the skyline like ribbon streamers." When we Koreans rushed out to see what was happening the Japanese police were very angry but they too looked at the sky with wonder. After the appearance of these planes blackouts were practiced more consistently and many residents of Seoul were forced to evacuate from the city, large numbers having to leave their possessions behind because of the limited transportation facilities.

News from the European and Pacific battlefields now brought grave concern to the Japanese. Germany and Italy were being defeated. American industrial plants were rolling out tanks, trucks, jeeps and planes endlessly and pouring them onto the battlefields. The tide had at last turned. Hitler and Mussolini were nearly done for and the Japanese were losing their war in Leyte, Iwo Jima, Okinawa. However, the Japanese never admitted defeat but said they were retreating for "military purposes." Since all the radios which had more than three tubes had been taken away from us, we could not often get the outside news.

But the B-29's dropping bombs on the main islands of Japan could not be hidden. They were too close to be screened. Not only that, but the looks of the Japanese people betrayed that they must be at a dead end. They had the appearance of an already defeated people. In May, 1945, V-E Day came. Then during the first part of August, 1945, the A-bombs were dropped, first on Hiroshima and then on Nagasaki, followed by Russia's declaration of war on Japan. The hope of the Japanese people seemed literally suffocated.

All this while our entire nation had been living on rations. Moreover the allotments per person were never filled. We were supposed to get two and a half handfuls of rice per person each day but we never got the full amount. Sugar was to be doled out at the rate of four ounces per person every six months but many were not lucky enough to get any sugar at all. Our family got none. As to meat, we Koreans were entirely without it except as we were able to use bribery on the quiet. All the cattle had been slaughtered to feed the Japanese troops. Even fresh vegetables were scarce. The farmers had such a huge quota to meet that they rarely had anything left for the markets, and if they did they had no time to take their produce to the villages, not to mention the fact that their footgear had given out and they had no time to make more. Transportation was only possible for the Japanese; they had conscripted every vehicle for their own purposes. Coffee and tea were a very great luxury and therefore entirely out of reach for many, but they were not our national beverages and we thanked our Lord that rice water (*sungnung*) was nearly always available. At pickling time there was a huge exodus of women from the cities to the farms, bringing with them all sorts of merchandise to use in bartering. For cabbages, turnips and fresh greens they offered cloth, soap, oil for cooking, and every conceivable item to tempt the farmer into parting with his fresh produce. What a babel it was. Excitement ran high. All in all many satisfactory transactions took place.

The practice of Japanese *misogi,* fasting and meditating, began. Groups of teachers, leaders and officials went to quiet places such as temples and stayed two or three days, sitting on their knees, forgetting all their physical needs and trying to put themselves in rapport with the Eternal One who could enlighten and invigorate them. They had only one bowl of thin porridge three times a day; they were taken out and stripped of their clothing and doused with cold water and then marched round and round to be awakened from drowsiness in meditation. With many the practice was an act; they felt forced to conform to this traditional method of meeting an emergency. But some were in earnest and if their purposes as individuals and as a nation had been pure, they might have been answered.

The Korean Christians went underground, as has been the way in time of necessity since the days of Nero. Many, however, were imprisoned. All of us felt we were buried in a tomb. But there had to be a resurrection and we were waiting for that day. How significant it was that the pioneer Christian missionary, H. G. Appenzeller of the Methodists, had arrived in Korea on Easter Sunday in 1885! Now there were about 600,000 Christians of all denominations, including the Catholics. I knew they were all praying toward one end—justice, liberty, peace. When the faith of all these Christians was added together something was bound to happen.

About a year before the war ended Mother became ill. She had never been ill before, even with a common cold or ordinary aches or pains. She had often said, "If I ever get sick I will die." Now she was eighty-five years old by the Korean calendar. Because of the shortage of food during the war there was first illness among the very old and very young, since those who were of productive age were given the preference in the amount of food issued. Many old people and children were dying. Mother knew that lack of food was the cause of her illness. Nevertheless she insisted that the girls, Iris and Lotus, have her share. When our little family ate together she always gave them the most consideration. I was anxious to have her consult some doctors, but she refused, knowing that the end was near. For three months she was up and down, yet she never complained. When asked if she had any pain she always assured us with a smile that she was not suffering. She yearned to be able to worship with her friends in the Christian church but she was not able.

Two weeks before she died she said, "I want to walk all

around the house while I am still able," for she knew she could not hold out much longer. She loved every nook and cranny of that house as she had taken good care of it, polishing and cleaning and giving it her loving attention. So I helped her from her bed and supported her on the little tour of inspection. Her dogs, Elsie and Mary, which she loved so well, followed her and she played with them and said to me, "Please don't let the dog hunters kill them but take care of them until they die a natural death." To her they had been a great source of joy. She loved to have them greet her upon returning home.

One day she said, "I am so hungry for a bit of fresh fish." It was summer and therefore very difficult to get fresh fish because of the lack of refrigeration, but after a great deal of effort I finally obtained one small fish which I divided into three parts, serving one part raw, one part in soup, and the third part broiled. Although she usually just nibbled a bit, this time she enjoyed these servings of fish to the full.

Toward the end she called to me, saying that she wanted me to hear her last prayer. It was thus: "Dear Father, thank you for the long and happy life you have given me and for the wonderful way you have taken care of me. Thank you most of all for your beloved Son, Jesus Christ. I have made many mistakes but you know that I did not mean to, and I ask your forgiveness. Thank you too for my son-girl who has been such a joy to me. Bless her and her two girls in the days and years to come and give them Thy blessing in all their undertakings for Thee."

After resting a while she decided that she wanted to sing some of the old Korean folk songs and some hymns she had loved so much, and so we sang together the simple folk song,

"I'm going away, leaving you behind, but never think I will forget you forever." Next, her favorite hymn, which was

> My Jesus, as thou wilt!
> All shall be well for me;
> Each changing future scene
> I gladly trust with thee.
> Straight to my home above
> I travel calmly on,
> And sing, in life or death,
> "My Lord, thy will be done."

Then she wanted to see the grass-linen shroud, such as all the common people wear, which she had made herself so as not to trouble anyone when the time came for her to wear it. When I brought it from her chest she said, "I wonder how I will look in it." After musing a while she continued, "What is death after all to a Christian but slipping into God's presence?"

Mother and I had often discussed together her funeral and burial plans. She dreaded the idea of cremation; for one thing it was a Japanese custom and for another she thought of her resurrection as physical. But she had never approved of the inconvenience, the great financial obligation, and the loss of time involved in ceremonial rites which would be necessary by following the old Confucian burial method. A burial lot had to be carefully chosen when a grandfather or father died, for it was believed that the future fortune and happiness of the deceased's family depended upon the location and type of soil in which he was buried. A burial site must face south and be surrounded by hills of a certain contour. Consequently some of the most beautiful and desirable spots were occupied by the dead. All of these customs she had rejected, of course, upon becoming a Christian. And her practical turn of mind was obvious in her final conclusion: "I am not going to crowd the living people with my dead body. Cremate me. I want to be helpful even with my physical tabernacle." She was content with her decision.

Mother died on August 31, 1944, in her sleep.

Ordinarily burial takes place about three days after death but with the heat of summer and difficulties of the times it was decided to have a small, quiet funeral within twenty-four hours, with her Christian pastor in charge. When the little party arrived at the crematory beyond West Gate, which was run by the Japanese, they found forty bodies ahead of them awaiting cremation. This delay was due to a lack of fuel.

As I reviewed Mother's life I realized what a wonderful woman she had been. She had belonged to the traditional life of old Korea but ever since she had caught the new vision in the Christian Church—that women were individuals—she had been determined to give her daughter an opportunity to learn, in order that she might lead Korean women to a fuller and richer life, and through the women to help Korean men also, for if the Korean women were better educated they would raise the standard of family life. I was proud to be my mother's daughter. I had an obligation to work for her ideals. I recalled what she had said about the new Korea coming out of the birth pangs of the war years. I saluted her spirit. "Dear Mother, so be it." We would not weep for her, nor even for ourselves; but our days, our hearts and our house had many lonely corners.

14

Liberation

It was August 15, 1945. I had invited two friends to have some Korean noodles for lunch. In those days it was a treat to be invited out and Iris and Lotus prepared a good lunch. We were enjoying pleasant conversation, with the radio turned on so that we might catch the news, when the announcer said to stand by for there would be an important announcement. In a few seconds a very grave voice, trembling, announced that Japan had surrendered unconditionally to the Allied Forces. It was the emperor of Japan speaking! At first we were stunned. Then we all stood up, holding hands, and shouted. However, we soon became very circumspect for we were still surrounded by the Japanese police. Walking out into the courtyard we looked over the walls to see what was happening on the street. Nothing was happening. People were walking about without any sign of excitement. I thought perhaps we had not understood the Japanese announcement or had misconstrued what had been said, but in a short while friends dropped by and assured us the news was as we had heard it. Finally taking in the full import of the emperor's statement, we felt as though the heavy iron gate of a prison had opened, setting us free after thirty-five years. I wished that my mother were here with us to see the beautiful dawn of the new era she had helped to bring to pass.

Happily we cried, "Now no more Japanese language!" Among the common people this language barrier had proved a great wall, separating parents from their children. Lustily we sang the Korean national anthem to the tune of "Auld Lang Syne." No more Japanese names would be forced on us. Paradoxically, after our liberation, some Japanese waitresses in restaurants changed to Korean names.

But actually our joy was mitigated with remorse, with grief, thinking of Hiroshima. I remember a fine Japanese Christian who lived in our neighborhood saying at the beginning of the war, "When I heard that the Japanese had dropped bombs on Pearl Harbor, I wept." Now I understood what she had meant. After the atomic bombs were dropped on Japan this same Japanese friend said, "This is the result of our dropping bombs on Pearl Harbor. Why can't we find a sensible way to settle our differences instead of dropping bombs on each other? Why don't we venture to use a more powerful bomb than all of these explosives—the bomb of prayer?" Her husband was also a Christian and the representative of American Mentholatum which had a wide distribution in Korea. Through everything we had Japanese Christian friends.

Handbills were soon dropped from planes by the United States Army advising the people that the 24th Corps, headed by Lt. Gen. John R. Hodge, would soon come into Seoul to liberate the Korean people from the Japanese. Eagerly we awaited their arrival.

On August 9, 1945 (Korean time), six days before the surrender, Russia had declared war on Japan, and the Russian Army had entered North Korea on the 11th, so that when the

Japanese capitulated the Russians were already in that area. In order to expedite matters, the 38th parallel was designated as a temporary line of demarcation north of which the Russian Army should receive the Japanese surrender and south of which the United States should act. During the interval between the announcement of the surrender on August 15 and the arrival of the United States troops in South Korea on September 9, the Russian Army was actively carrying on communistic activity in North Korea. In the South committees preparing to establish an independent Korea were organized by certain Korean leaders and patriots, including released political prisoners. We noted that these leaders seemed to be of the leftist persuasion and we wondered how such efficient organization could spring up overnight. Later we found out that the Communists had prepared for this time long before Japan had surrendered and these organizations had been carefully trained. Almost immediately a National Congress was convened in Seoul, attended by representatives from all over Korea. On September 6, the People's Republic was proclaimed, three days before the United States Army came into South Korea. We felt it strange that this proclamation was issued before the American Armed Forces arrived. The Japanese authorities were afraid both of the Russians and of the Korean people but they granted authority to the Russian Army, even extending some special favors to enhance their position with them. The Russian Army did not stop at the 38th parallel but crossed over into South Korea, even looting south of this line.

Finally the 24th Corps of the United States Army landed at Inchon and marched into Seoul, announcing their coming through newspapers and over the radio as well as in leaflets dropped from planes. The twenty-five-mile route from Inchon to Seoul was lined with people waving Korean and American flags. As I stood near the Capitol in Seoul and watched the well-fed, smartly uniformed soldiers as they rolled into the city with their impressive equipment, I was deeply moved. Their open, smiling faces showed no signs of weariness or bitterness. They were different from any soldiers we had ever seen. When they reached the city they took over all of the important buildings, both government and civic; also the big stores, factories and other Japanese-owned institutions.

As soon as the American Armed Forces occcupied the city the People's Republic offered their services but the American leaders, knowing how this government had been organized, declined their offer, saying that the American Military Government in South Korea was the only legal government. The real leaders of South Korean political and civic groups, totaling about three hundred, were called together by Lt. Gen. Hodge at the City Hall to confer with him and his staff. I was one of this group. Among other things, he assured us that "the United States wishes to see a united, independent and democratic Korean government established as early as possible and has made solemn commitments to aid the Korean people to achieve their independence. This is the sole reason why Americans are in Korea." Welcome speeches were made by various Korean leaders and each expressed joy and gratitude and offered good wishes to America from Korea. Everyone returned to his or her work after the period of excitement was over and it never occurred to us that there would be a division of our country into North and South Korea.

Now the repatriation of the Japanese began. The Japanese Army was disbanded and the soldiers and civilian population were sent back home. They were allowed to take only a certain amount of personal belongings with them. By hundreds they moved out; even those in North Korea and Manchuria traveled through South Korea on their way to Japan. For the most part they traveled on foot, emaciated, hungry and inadequately clothed. At the same time Korean forced laborers were returning home to Korea from Japan. The women's organizations did a magnificent job of helping these moving masses.

The United States Military Government, headed by the late Gen. Archer L. Lerch, directed the redivision of large estates owned by the Japanese and the selling of the smaller farms to the Koreans who had lost them. Factories, forests, mines, farms and fishing rights which had been in the hands of the Japanese were taken over by the American Military Government. Most exciting of all was the freedom of speech, press and religion given to our people who had so long been denied these human rights.

For the first flag-raising ceremony hundreds of my fellow countrymen gathered around the beautiful marble Capitol on a fine October day. United States troops stood at attention while their band played the Korean national anthem and two young Koreans officiated at the flagpole. I watched our flag go up inch by inch, foot by foot, until it reached the top of the pole where it slowly unfurled against the bright blue of the sky. How beautiful it looked with its snow-white ground, upon the center of which was a red and blue sphere representing "Yang" and "Um," which symbolizes the pairs of complementary forces in all nature, with black trigrams on each of the four corners representing philosophical conceptions understood by the people. This was the flag of old Korea formally adopted by the Republic of Korea. It touched me deeply to see the respect shown by the American officers and soldiers. I realized how much this day had cost in human life, how many battles had been fought and how much precious blood had been shed to allow us once again to fly our flag as a free people.

Almost immediately political parties arose, fifty-four of them, including five major parties and one women's party. Why so many? Because the people had been denied civil rights for so long; now they exercised their right to form parties as a way of showing their independence. However, experience soon taught us that we must unite into fewer but stronger parties. During this stage, Syngman Rhee arrived from America, and next came Kim Koo—one of our great patriots in exile— and his followers from China. While they met and discussed policy an average of two thousand North Korean refugees streamed daily into South Korea to escape the new Soviet regime. Into my home came friends and relatives, and friends of relatives. Once a family of five—mother, father and three girls—stayed a week, having come all the way from Antung, Manchuria. They had left all of their possessions behind, so we shared what we had. Every refugee realized one thing—each must earn his own rice, otherwise he would die. So the whole family went out to look for work; the mother and the two youngest girls bought apples and resold them; the oldest girl got a job through a friend in the U. S. Army office; the father found work in a place where a house was being repaired. They rented one room near by and moved into it. Never in our history had men, women and children become as rice-earning conscious as they were now. Heretofore the head of the family had had the sole responsibility for all the members of the family and often for poor relatives as well. But now a new order was coming into actuality; the democratic way of life was the child of necessity and it had great appeal.

Refugees brought reports that the Russians were stripping North Korean factories and shipping the equipment to Russia. Also that the Russian Army came in and ate the food which the Japanese had stored for their Army and that the food which they could not eat was being sent to Russia. In contrast, when the American Army had come into South Korea they had brought their food with them with an extra allotment to feed the hungry. The Russians also had set up their own form of government in North Korea and had requisitioned all farms over four or five acres and placed North Korean tenants on them, but later they demanded the harvest and in the end the tenants had nothing in return for their labor. It was said that the people were so suppressed that nothing was heard but footsteps. On the other hand, the voices of the South Koreans were raised loudly in free discussion.

The next step in the carrying out of the commitment for a united and independent Korea was a three-power conference in Moscow in December, 1945. According to the Cairo Conference held in November, 1943, the United States, Great Britain and China had agreed to Korean independence "in due course"; now the United States, the United Kingdom and the U. S. S. R. promised independence according to the Cairo agreement but "not yet." Instead of immediate independence, a trusteeship would be set up for the next five years. The explanation given was that Korea had been under Japanese domination for so long that the people must be trained to take over the reins of government. When this news came out, most Koreans were opposed to the edict as we wanted immediate self-government. The next day the Communist party came out in favor of trusteeship.

When the Soviet-American Joint Commission met in Seoul

to make suitable plans for setting up a unified government, the first problem was to decide who among the Korean leaders should be consulted. The U. S. delegation suggested that all political parties be given an opportunity to have their say while the Russian delegation insisted that only those who were in favor of trusteeship should be consulted. The U. S. delegation insisted that this was not democratic procedure so no agreement was reached. Henceforth all attempts to set up a unified, independent government failed. In an effort to break this stalemate the American Military Government appealed to the U. N. Political and Security Council to expedite the formation of the proposed unified government.

There was a friendly feeling between the American Military forces and the Korean people. No matter where the American G. I.'s went, they immediately made friends with the children. Although they had come directly from the battlefront, they always seemed to be well supplied with goodies, such as chocolate bars, chewing gum and bubble gum which they gave to the boys and girls, even teaching them how to blow the gum bubbles. This kindness to children warmed the hearts of the nationals and they realized that these men had come from a child-centered country. The children soon learned how to say "okay, okay" and "hello, hello," as these words had no sound difficulty for a Korean tongue. Often companies of soldiers adopted orphans as their mascots, feeding and clothing them, and teaching them to speak English. Frequently these boys became interpreters.

Friendliness between Americans and Koreans abounded. One day a young American lieutenant came to our gate and asked for me. When I greeted him he said, "This is Joey, Mrs. Bailey's son." Then he explained, "When you came to speak at my mother's school, Dwight School in Englewood, New Jersey, I was a little fellow, but you said to me, 'Who knows, you may come to see me in Korea when you grow up.' And now I have come to help liberate your Korea."

Sometimes the methods of communication between Koreans and the American soldiers were most amusing. Many Korean women laundered the soldiers' clothing, receiving in return such commodities as candy, cigarettes and soap. One day a woman came to a barracks to get a bundle of clothing to be washed. The soldier wanted to tell her that he wished to have his laundry back in three days, so he held up three fingers, one after the other. She nodded, then looking up at the sky as though scanning for rain, she twinkled her fingers like rain falling while making the sound *"r-r-r-r,"* and lifted her fourth finger to indicate that if it rained she would bring it back the fourth day. Pantomime served its purpose.

The soldiers were invariably considerate of women and girls. If they were traveling on village roads and saw women carrying heavy loads on their heads or babies on their backs, and sometimes small children at their sides as well, the soldiers almost always gave them a ride if space permitted. Or if the soldiers encountered stranded motor cars, whether military equipment or the property of some Koreans, they usually stopped to investigate. One day I was riding to Yancoke when the car stopped and refused to start. A G. I. came along in a jeep, stopped, looked the car over, discovered it was out of gasoline, took gas from the tank of his jeep and transferred it to the car. These boys seemed equal to any emergency.

They also showed great respect for human life, whether man, woman or child. For example, there was a fire near my home and a person was known to be trapped inside. G. I.'s used

Army fire-fighting equipment and one soldier plunged into the blaze and saved the trapped individual. I recall another instance when a flood threatened a village near Sunwon and a soldier was commissioned to help the village people cross the bridge to safety. He stayed at his post until he was swept away by the flood waters and lost his own life. These and many other examples of heroism helped to create a new evaluation of human life among our people. Their sacrifices endeared Americans to us.

Naturally we Koreans watched the construction operations of the engineers with great interest, whether they were building Quonset huts, roads or airports. We noticed that when it came to establishing a base, living quarters for the soldiers were built before those of the officers. I remarked upon this fact one day to a Captain Van Deeven. He said, "Well, since the soldiers are the ones who do the fighting they should be taken care of first." To us this was a wonderful demonstration of the democratic way of life.

When it came to road building, bulldozers, scrapers and steam rollers were put into use and in no time miles of road were completed, covered with a hard surface of tar. Our old attempts at road building involved the use of a long-handled shovel with ropes attached, requiring three to five men for operation, one man pushing and filling the shovel while the others pulled it back by the ropes. The contrast in the mechanics involved was unbelievable. The Americans drove machines; the Koreans drove men. It would not take long to rebuild Korea by modern engineering methods if properly trained and organized workmen were available.

Another source of never-ending wonder was the fly and mosquito control program carried out by the American Army.

These pests abounded in summer and with lack of screens for the homes and poor sewage disposal, a critical health problem had developed. Then the Army came along with its D. D. T.! The sudden freedom from insects was almost as much of a miracle to us Koreans as our new-found freedom from Japanese oppression.

Almost immediately the school system was reorganized into the 6-3-3 plan: six years of grammar school, three of junior high school and three of senior high school. New textbooks were written in Korean, based upon democratic principles stressing the sacredness of human personality, in contrast to the Japanese teachings of militarism and the emperor man-god worship. Happily children learned to sing folk songs again, and played with democratic abandon. Once more the old Korean holidays were observed, long forbidden by the Japanese. Although there was little food available for the extra celebration of these holidays, the spirit of celebration prevailed.

Men and women now wore the kind and color of clothing they pleased, especially white which had been forbidden by the Japanese on the pretext that white clothing was uneconomical. The Japanese in the market places had been known to throw ink upon Korean men or women if they dressed in white. Local industries were again developed, such as the making of boxes of inlaid mother-of-pearl, Korean flags, brasswork of new design, brassbound teakwood chests, rubber shoes, embroidery work of beautiful design and workmanship. Time was once more found for painting and the composing of music. In Seoul there were two excellent symphony orchestras; the National Theater presented Korean and Chinese drama; a truly fine opera company produced *Carmen*.

Through all of these new developments we were constantly

bombarded with propaganda by the Communists who were making the most of freedom of speech, press and organization for accomplishing their own goals. They condemned any Koreans who had ever found it necessary to deal with the Japanese for any reason, calling them traitors and creating suspicion among Koreans. The only way to meet Communist propaganda was to outdo it with democratic propaganda, including the doctrine that "bygones should be bygones" and that from the time of Liberation everyone's conduct would be judged from that day on.

When the American Military Government announced that women would have the franchise if they prepared themselves to exercise this right, we educated women determined that we would do everything possible to prepare our sex for this new privilege. I was chairman of the Political Education Committee of the Patriotic Women's Society and at once became deeply involved in arranging classes for women who would be eligible to vote when the time came.

Women police were also organized for the first time in Korean history and with smart-looking uniforms and suitable training they were able to do a great deal to help the women and children. They were captained by a friend of mine, Gladys Koh, who had also attended Wesleyan College in Georgia. Sometimes they directed the traffic along with policemen and it gave them great delight to stop male pedestrians by simply stretching out their hands. On the whole they were very conscientious but once the captain admitted to me that remembering the many centuries during which men had given all of the orders, she sometimes held her hand outstretched a shade longer than necessary and received in return many harsh looks from the men who passed by after she had given the "Go" signal. With great glee I watched her do this. Could you blame us for enjoying such a situation?

Several groups were sent to America to observe democracy on its home field. The first group was comprised of doctors, the second group of teachers. Some American colleges gave scholarships to Korean students through the American Military Government, the Government selecting the recipients. When the director of the Korean Department of Education announced that the Department would send two Korean girls to America to study, my daughter Lotus was recommended by her college as a candidate. Competitive examinations were to be given, and when Lotus asked me for some idea as to what those examinations might cover I named three possibilities: English language, general intelligence, adaptability and poise. Then I summed up my advice in four words: "Use your common sense." Lotus took the examinations and received the scholarship. When I asked her about her experience she told me that the committee was made up of five Americans and one Korean. When she entered the examination room the members were seated and there was one vacant chair. After a moment's silence she asked, "May I be seated?" Somebody said, "Of course," and one of the American gentlemen helped her to be seated. She was thrilled with this courtesy which seemed a sign of the new times.

From the time the American Army came in, worship services were conducted on Sunday mornings by Chaplain Morton Hickman in the Throne Room of the Capitol and I played the organ for these services. It was a portable reed organ which the G. I.'s had found somewhere in a broken-down condition and had repaired. At the same time another service was held at the First Methodist Church in Chungdong. When I remembered that the Throne Room had never before been used by any except high officials and when I saw American soldiers coming in to worship along with the Korean people, I realized the true meaning of democracy. These Sunday meetings grew by leaps and bounds until there was not even standing room.

All of these things which were happening throughout my country convinced me that the United States was sincere in her democratic principles and concern for human welfare, Red propaganda to the contrary. This conviction was deepened when the Philippines were given their independence on July 4, 1946, as promised in 1934 by the Tydings-McDuffie Act. We Koreans were so moved that we held a celebration, erecting a congratulatory gate of pine branches in Seoul on the main thoroughfare leading to the Capitol. We were now sure that the United States kept its promises and we looked forward to the time of our own complete liberation.

In December I was invited to become a radio lecturer in the Political Education Section of the Department of Public Information of the American Military Government. I accepted because I realized that Korean women needed this education to prepare themselves for the franchise. I wrote a series of fifteen-minute speeches on different subjects, emphasizing the Korean woman's responsibility for democracy, and I delivered one talk each week. I was also invited to speak to the G. I.'s stationed in Seoul and vicinity once or twice a week, and at the clubs conducted by the American Red Cross. I entertained G. I.'s and Red Cross friends in my home, giving them a glimpse of Korean home life. Together we took trips to historical sites, to Buddhist temples and to Yangcoke to show the Americans different phases of our life. Some time later when speaking on various American campuses I met a number of my former G. I. friends. J. E. Fisher, an American friend of long standing, and Henry D. Appenzeller, son of the first Methodist missionary to Korea, also worked in the Political Education Section. For my radio work I received a special citation from the Military Governor, Gen. Archer L. Lerch, along with thirteen other Koreans, one woman and twelve men, all of whom worked with the American Military Government.

Of all the experiences we Koreans had during the liberation perhaps the first Easter Sunrise Service was the climax. Before dawn thousands of Korean Christians lighted their candles, lanterns or flashlights and began to climb up Namsan which is crowned at the top by a beautiful Shinto shrine. As the Christians climbed the last three hundred and fifty steps they sang together, "Up from the grave He arose . . . with a mighty triumph o'er His foes." Just as they arrived at the top of the mountain, dawn broke and the Easter morning sun came up above the pines. People could scarcely sing for weeping. But they sang! Christ was indeed risen from the dead. There were hundreds of American G. I.'s and officers at that service, which was conducted both in Korean and English. I regret to this day that I was unable to be present on that historic and impressive Easter morning but Iris was ill. However, I caught the spirit of the service, as did thousands, both Christians and non-Christians.

During this period Iris, my oldest daughter, became engaged. Both girls had graduated from Ewha College, Iris as a music major and Lotus in English. Iris and I were the first mother-daughter pair thus to graduate from Ewha and made the first record of its kind in Korean history. After graduation she taught music in Dukwha and Ewha High School, and Lotus worked in a library. As the girls grew to young womanhood my

first concern was with their marriage. My mother and I saw
eye to eye on that point. Knowing the old traditional way in
which my mother and grandmother had been married and the
headstrong manner in which I had managed my own marriage,
I wanted to help them marry well and happily. I again recalled
the old Korean proverb, "The life of your daughter and the
course of a stream depend on what you do to guide them." I
decided to evolve a new marriage pattern for my girls to follow.
When the proper time came we elders were to choose suitors
for them but allow the girls a final decision. We elders were to
learn the background, education, health, temperament and
character of the young man in question without emotion or
biased judgment. If we thought the young couple would be
compatible we would let them get acquainted and decide the
issue for themselves. It was the best method we could reason
out in that transitional period of Korea's development. Young
people did not have many opportunities to meet by themselves,
and dating was very rare. If there was dating, it was done
under cover. And so I acquainted my girls with these plans for
them.

Iris' turn came first, being the eldest. I sensed she was beginning to be interested in a certain young man. She had every
right to be interested in men, yet socially in Korea it did not
sound quite proper to hear that so-and-so's daughter "went
with" a young man without the approval of her people. I asked
Iris if she had any particular young man in mind that she really
cared for. She answered, "Yes, I have one." You can imagine the
feeling I had when she gave me such a positive answer! Now
I realized what a shock it must have been to my mother when
I told her of my choosing a husband for myself.

I decided to handle this situation with care and inquired how

and where she had met him, what family he was from, and
what he was doing. All this without antagonizing her feelings.
In case the young man should not prove to be a proper person
for her, I would have to deflect her interest tactfully. But I
found that the young man came from a good family with
considerable wealth. He was studying to be a physician, which
was a much needed profession in Korea. She had met him at
his grandmother's home when she was giving piano lessons
to his sister, a student of Ewha. The only objection I had to him
was his temperament. He was quick and nervous. Iris was
inclined to be nervous too. I did not see how two nervous
people could navigate their married life smoothly. She had need
of a man who was dependable, calm and understanding. I knew
then that I ought to find a better man than this one and intro-
duce him to her.

So Iris' youngest aunt and I found another young man, Lee
Sang-Hak, whom we thought would be proper for her and
presented him to her casually. He was a brother of one of my
former students and a graduate of a college in Japan. He had
suffered imprisonment in Seoul as an anti-Japanese when he
was a senior in high school. His and Iris' zodiacal signs indicated
great compatibility, he being a horse and she a dog. His family
and ours provided different occasions for their meeting and so
the members of both families became acquainted also. It is
necessary for the uncles and aunts and grandparents, if alive,
to be consulted, for in Korea family life is horizontal. The in-
laws are attached by the newly married couple. In America
family life is vertical; the young husband and wife are detached
from their respective families and form a new family unit. I
presume that this is the reason the young people in America

find their own suitors and get their parents' approval, whereas in Korea it is the reverse.

For three months we guided Iris and Sang-Hak, then allowed the stream to follow its own course. One day Iris confided to me what a splendid young man Sang-Hak was! She said, "He is very considerate and understanding. He is of far better caliber than the young medical man. He has never studied music, but at least he is trying to show his appreciation of it. I am doing the same toward his interests."

I was happy to be able to say, "Well, Iris, our plan has worked."

She replied, "Yes, it has. You couldn't have chosen any better man. He is for me."

These two young folks were actually in love—just as we elders had hoped them to be. What a relief it was for us, with no issue involved. From now on there should be smooth sailing!

The wedding date was set. It was to be on November 24. Just a month before the wedding Iris came down with a high temperature. The doctor was called in and after examining her carefully he said she should rest for at least six months. It was a serious case of nervous exhaustion. When her fiance was advised of the doctor's recommendation he did not say a word, but the next day he brought a bottle of vitamin B complex to be given hypodermically and for three months he came every day after his work to see her and give her an injection of vitamins. Eventually she became entirely well and the long-postponed wedding took place the following year.

One day during Iris' convalescence Helen Nixon, a Red Cross worker who had helped to organize the women's department of the Military Government, came to my office to say that her department had received an invitation for a Korean woman to represent Korea at the First International Assembly of Women being held in the United States. The group was to meet in South Kortright, New York, where they would study the status of women in relation to human rights all over the world. However, Mrs. Nixon explained that there were two complications in the invitation; first, that there was no money available for expenses, and second, the time was so limited that whatever was done had to be done quickly. She explained that $3,000 would be required because the fare by air would be $1,000 each way and another thousand would be necessary for living expenses for three months. Then she asked, "Could you go?"

"I have five dollars," was my reply. "How long do I have to find the other $2,995?"

"Today is Wednesday. We will have to know by Friday."

I enjoy working on such a problem and in three days, through my loyal friends, the necessary financial arrangements were made. The American Military Government issued my passport but my visa was denied by the Supreme Commander for the Allied Powers in Tokyo because with the division of Korea they could not send me as an official representative of all Korea. I did not give up. I applied again for a visa as an observer instead of a representative. The next day it came through. Much to my disappointment there was no seat available on the Army transport plane and in those days no commercial air liners were available in Korea.

On Tuesday, October 6, which was the deadline for my trip to the First International Assembly of Women, an American soldier came to my office and asked, "Is Mrs. Pack here?" I laughed, "Mrs. Pack is not here but Mrs. Pahk is."

In a nonchalant way he replied, "Well, Mrs. Pack, Pock, Park, or whatever your name is, you are scheduled to fly to America on the plane leaving at noon today."

I was overwhelmed with surprise and joy. I rushed home in Dr. Appenzeller's car and grabbed my twenty-one-inch suitcase and went to the Kimpo Airport fifteen miles from Seoul. When I arrived the passenger list was being checked. A major had canceled his reservation at the last minute and consequently that seat was left for me. Korean women were to be represented at the First International Assembly of Women since the war!

15

Korea becomes Known

In four hours we arrived in Tokyo. It was just before dinner-time. Betty Alt, a former missionary then working with the United States Army in Japan, met me at the airport and took me to the women's quarters where I was billeted over-night. During this brief stopover I could see that Japan, defeated fourteen months previously, was showing signs of recovery. The devastation of war had been cleared away and the rigid militaristic atmosphere had softened to a spirit of friendliness and comradeship. Young people walked hand in hand along the streets. The people had a well-groomed look even though their clothing was often worn. Numerous Japanese bootblacks were kept busy shining the G. I. shoes, apparently vying with one another to do a good job. Elevator attendants and Japanese waitresses in the dining hall which the army personnel used showed quiet courtesy and a desire to give their best service. Such a spirit of co-operation could not fail to help the Japanese make a good comeback.

As I was leaving the women's quarters a Japanese cleaning maid asked me in Japanese, "Are you going to America?" When I told her that was my destination she looked at me earnestly, almost pathetically, and said, "You are lucky! I wish that I could go too!" In spite of their defeat the younger generation of Japanese considered America the land of freedom, opportunity and plenty.

From Tokyo the plane took us in an almost straight line, bearing south a little, over fifteen hundred miles to Guam, the farthest outpost of the United States and an American possession since the Spanish-American War. Two Red Cross workers and I were put up in the women's quarters but were not allowed to walk into the surrounding country on account of danger from guerrilla attacks. I found that my suitcase, checked in Tokyo, had not traveled with me, but a cable to Miss Alt brought it the next morning just before we left.

At Guam I changed from the army transport to a Pan-American plane coming from Shanghai via Manila, which route had reopened only three weeks previous. One of the passengers was a Chinese, an important representative of his country, bound for the United States. As we flew over the blue Pacific toward Wake, following the regular China Clipper route, I talked with my fellow passenger, the first Chinese I had met since the liberation of my people. We discussed the 38th parallel and the problems it represented and he said, "It is not right that Korea is occupied by two forces. I think Russia was given too much at the Yalta Conference. She got everything she had planned to get out of the war—Port Arthur, Dairen, the Manchurian railways, Sakhlin and the Kurile Islands—yet she did the least to help win the war. Each of these places is of critical importance, geographically and economically. Take Port Arthur; it is the terminus of the Trans-Siberian railroad besides being an ice-free port on the Yellow Sea, well protected by rocky hills.

Dairen is another strategic Manchurian port. And Sakhlin. Russia first got that island back in 1875 in an exchange with Japan when the Japanese got the Kurile Islands. Then in 1905 you recall that Japan took back Sakhlin, largely because of its valuable coal, petroleum and fur-bearing animals. But Russia got back Sakhlin at Yalta along with the thirty-one Kuriles, rich in timber, fur and fish." He spoke gravely. Then in conclusion he added, "Mrs. Pahk, your problem is nothing compared to what we have to face."

We reached Wake—another United States possession—in time for dinner. From the air these three coral islands appeared to float on the ocean like lotus pads. I had the strange feeling that I could easily be washed off their low shores and drowned. After dinner we took off for the Midway Islands, 1,200 miles distant, which also belong to the United States. Coming from impoverished Korea I was impressed at each of these Pacific outposts with the fact that the American soldiers were well fed, well housed and well cared for, with movies and other amusements to sustain their morale.

The plane from Tokyo to Guam had been well filled with passengers but from Guam on there were only ten—two Orientals, and the rest Americans, mostly Army personnel. The trip from Midway to Hickam Field, Honolulu, was made overnight. Then I boarded a Pan-American Constellation for San Francisco, a hop of 2,100 miles, the longest of the trip. Arriving in San Francisco I was met by my good friend, Mrs. Yang, and her son-in-law, and she insisted on my spending the night at her home. The next morning I boarded a plane for New York. That evening as our plane approached the metropolitan area the sea of lights amazed me. In America, after all the horrors of war, the lights were still blazing, signalizing a haven to all who came from war-torn lands. A Korean friend put me on a bus bound for South Kortright. The autumn foliage was in its glory and I enjoyed every minute of the ride.

When I arrived in South Kortright I found sixty-seven American women and one hundred and nine women from overseas gathered together on a large estate for the First International Assembly of Women since the war. With only one day of the conference left, I registered as an onlooker-representative of the forty-eighth country, and even with as late an appearance as this, I was not the last, since a Hungarian lady registered as the forty-ninth.

The last meeting of the Assembly was to be held in the Waldorf-Astoria Hotel in New York. Chartered buses transported the delegates, stopping at Hyde Park to visit the Roosevelt estate. There we were welcomed graciously and cordially by Mrs. Roosevelt who served tea, after which we paid our respects to the late President at his grave. Also we visited the Roosevelt Library and Museum. In the museum I searched carefully among the gifts from all over the world for something from my own land, and sure enough, in a conspicuous place, along with gifts from China and Japan, I found a brass finger bowl and plate, chopsticks and spoon, a pair of miniature shoes, and a turtle-shaped paperweight. One of the group remarked, "What fine quality the Korean brass has." Of course I was happy to hear such a comment.

The next day I attended the final session of the Assembly. The program included the finding of the conference on the topic "The World We Live In—The World We Want." I noted that national representatives from China, India and Japan were listed for fifteen-minute speeches. No speaker was listed for Korea. Here I had spent nearly a thousand dollars to travel the 8,000 miles to this meeting and I felt a definite responsibility to let this great group of women know that Korea was represented. I wrote a note asking the chairman for a minute to speak before the Assembly. The return message read: "I'm very sorry; we're behind schedule and even a minute is impossible." I did not give up hope that I might be heard but I did not know how it could be arranged. More than two hours later just before the end of the morning session, I was asked to come to the platform. I reached it almost instantly. The chairman introduced me, and I said, "Friends, this is my third trip to the United States of America. On the first two trips I came as a Japanese subject, but today I come as a liberated Korean. I thank all of you who have helped to make this possible." I said what I had wanted to say in less than thirty seconds and I shall never forget the cheer which arose from the group.

The next day fifty of us delegates were invited to attend a weekend conference sponsored by the Intercultural Committee of the United Nations Council of Philadelphia. There were two public meetings, one for adults in Temple University and the other for high school representatives and teachers in Philadelphia High School for Girls. I was scheduled to speak for ten minutes with five other nationals to the student group. I told them about the G. I.'s, how they had made friends with our children, and something about the life of the average Korean boy and girl. I was thrilled with their wholehearted response, their enthusiastic interest toward my beloved country, and promised to return soon.

In my mail at Philadelphia was a letter from Maude-Louise Strayer of Dobbs Ferry, New York, asking me to address the girls of her school. I had met Miss Strayer at a Northfield Girls' Conference during my Student Volunteer Movement travels and through her influence the Dobbs Ferry students had given me financial assistance in my Korean work, considering me one of their missionaries. Miss Strayer had been the last person to write me before World War II and the first to send me a message after the war. I was very happy to accept her invitation.

From Dobbs Ferry I went to the convention of the United Council of Church Women at Grand Rapids, Michigan. In attendance were about one thousand women from the Protestant churches of the United States. The nationals from China, Japan and the Philippines were the first to come since the war. On the second evening of the conference Mrs. Mary McLeod Bethune, president of Bethune-Cookman College in Daytona Beach, Florida, was scheduled to speak but she was unable to come, so I took her place. After the meeting one lady grasped my hand and said, "Oh, Mrs. Bethune, you were perfectly marvelous!" I received numerous invitations for speaking engagements and my time was well filled for several months ahead.

I returned to Philadelphia to speak in the high schools as I had promised, the first one being Beeber Junior High School. Here to my great surprise a carefully worked out exhibit of pictures, sketches and essays on Korea had been arranged for "Korea Day." A G. I., returned from Korea, carried a Korean flag and a student an American flag; the orchestra played the Korean national anthem. Each student brought a package for Korea, which included pencils, mittens, socks, soap and candy; the packages were deposited in boxes for shipment, and in addition each student also contributed eleven cents toward mailing charges. Altogether twenty-three boxes weighing eight hundred pounds were sent to Ewha High School where they were received with suitable ceremony. Surprisingly a man's suit in good condition was found in one of these boxes and the students suggested that it be given to their principal. He insisted that it be given to one of the teachers who had a greater need for it and so the lucky teacher became the best-dressed man in the school.

Wishing to show their appreciation in return, each student at Ewha made some gift, a piece of embroidery, a painting, a native doll, a little purse, and so on, and these gifts were then sent to Beeber Junior High School and put on display there. One outstanding article was a black satin cushion with a peony hand-embroidered in beautiful colors and inscribed with the words: "To our Beeber Junior High Friends in Philadelphia from Ewha High Friends in Seoul."

In my visits to the schools in Philadelphia I tried to take Korea into the classrooms and the boys and girls showed their interest in the life of the Korean people and responded to the needs of the school children of my homeland. It seemed as if they had newly discovered Korea, the country which had been concealed for so long under the shadow of Japan. Several other schools in Philadelphia also sent gifts to high schools in Seoul. This mutual interest carried over into the homes, churches and other circles in which these American and Korean students moved. I spoke in twenty-three public junior and senior high schools at that time.

In various colleges throughout the country I met many G.I.'s who had served in the Pacific area, had been helped by Christian nationals, and had become much interested in missions. A number of times former G. I.'s spoke to me on the street, usually asking if I were Korean, and when I said, "Yes, I am, but how did you know?" they answered that they had served in Korea and recognized my native dress.

Miss Woodford of the Florida Chain of Missionary Assemblies arranged for me to come to their series of meetings in late January and early February. During those four weeks I gave ninety-three talks at their missionary programs. More lectures in churches of various denominations, in colleges, universities, schools and clubs kept me busy until the end of May. In June I represented Korea at a convention of the World's Woman's Christian Temperance Union in Asbury Park, New Jersey. About two thousand women from all parts of the world assembled here and I marveled at their courage as they went steadily on with their program of education and appropriate legislation. As I traveled the highways I saw signs costing millions of dollars aimed at inducing more people to drink more, yet here were Christian women—wives, mothers and daughters—determined to combat this evil which drags down the moral fiber of men and women and has currently netted America four million alcoholics. Compassion and determination must ultimately win. How? Alcoholics Anonymous is one answer. But all of us have a responsibility and our concerted strength was symbolized at the first evening session when at a given signal each person in the room lifted a lighted electric torch, depicting the fact that with the unified efforts of all the members around the world, light must prevail. Along with other nationals from China and India I spoke on the subject, "The Eyes of the World are on the East." I told them that since the women of my country now had the franchise, the men asked us how they might get the women's vote, and we Christian women told them that if they drank they would *not* get our vote. At last women held a club.

I left the convention to go to Adelphi College, Garden City, New York, to deliver the commencement address, an especial pleasure for me since this was the college which had granted a scholarship to my daughter Lotus who was planning to arrive in late August. Just prior to going to Asbury Park, I had received a letter from Iris telling me that Lotus was ill. She had suffered a hemorrhage and it was believed that she might be suffering from tuberculosis. Previously Lotus had written she had not been feeling well; she was running a slight temperature each afternoon, which she thought might be a cold. But she reassured me that she would soon be better and join me as planned. I knew she was no doubt suffering from malnutrition endured in the war period. Many Koreans had died of malnutrition and thousands more would die before their time because of weakened constitutions. To be sure, that same condition existed in most of the occupied countries but that did not make it easier for each individual. I thought that the good care which Iris and the rest of the family would give her would soon put Lotus on her feet, for the young recover easily. Iris appeared to be of the same mind and advised me to continue with my schedule, promising to keep me posted. Nevertheless a burden of concern for Lotus lay heavily upon my heart.

From Adelphia College I went on to Lake Junaluska, North Carolina, where I stayed with Dr. and Mrs. Quillian. While there I received a cable: "LOTUS SERIOUSLY ILL STOP BRING STREPTOMYCIN STOP HURRY HOME IRIS." Somehow I got through my speech that evening, leaving with Mrs. Quillian immediately afterward to pack for my long journey. After I left the auditorium Dr. Quillian told the audience of my need for streptomycin, which cost six dollars a vial at that time. So ready was their response that their gifts totaled over three hundred dollars.

I traveled the 75 miles to Spartanburg, South Carolina, by taxi, provided by Dr. Quillian. There Dr. Greene, former dean of Georgia Wesleyan, and his wife put me on the train for Washington where I had to secure my papers. Purchasing a supply of streptomycin, I went on to my Ridgewood headquarters, the home of the Hardenberghs, and made final preparations, canceling all dates for the coming fall. Mrs. Hardenbergh, her mother and sister, and Mrs. K. K. Quimby, drove me to LaGuardia Airport. Mrs. Quimby, whose husband had been minister of the Ridgewood Methodist Church in that town, and Dr. Quillian together, raised the funds to cover my transportation back home. I was wonderfully blessed with generous and loyal friends!

On this tour I had traveled 30,000 miles and had made three hundred speeches. Again I was returning to my homeland with a great burden upon my heart. If only the miles could dissolve as a mist and I could find myself at my child's side!

16

Lotus

It was a Northwest Airliner I boarded at 6:00 P.M. on August 6, 1947, and flew to Minneapolis where I changed to another plane flying directly to the Orient via Alaska. There were fifteen passengers, including a little boy. Our first stop was Anchorage, where I had time to get off the plane and walk around this booming outpost of the United States. It was the seventh day of August but the air felt like a late fall day. I had never seen Eskimos before and when I discovered that they spoke English well I talked with them. They were standing near a drugstore eating ice cream cones in typical American fashion. When I asked them where they lived they told me their homes were in the Far North and that they were in Anchorage on a fishing trip. Since Eskimos and Orientals have similar features, being of common origin, they apparently took me for an Eskimo and in turn asked me where I lived. When I told them I was from Korea they said, "Where is Korea? Have never heard of it before." Since this was the farthest north I had ever traveled I was greatly interested in the midnight sun and when I asked how much farther north one must travel to see this phenomenon they told me several hundred miles.

From Anchorage we flew to Shemya Airport on the Aleutian Islands. Here it was cold, foggy and damp. We stayed only long enough to have dinner at the mess hall of the Officers' Club and then continued on our journey. Next came a forced landing on Adak, the extreme western island of the Aleutian chain. Here I overheard that General Eisenhower's plane had taken off the day before. This island is a neighbor to the islands of Attu and Kisha, where the Aleutian battles took place during World War II. A continued spell of bad weather forced us to spend the night on this island, and a young mother with her three-year-old boy and I were housed in the unoccupied Red Cross quarters which were kept intact for such emergency use. At 5:00 A. M. we continued our journey across the Pacific. The atmosphere was crystal clear, the ocean very beautiful, and now we could see dotted here and there the islands which had been invisible in the fog of the previous day. This was the final leg of our trip to Tokyo.

Because of the delay at Adak I missed my connection with the plane from Tokyo to Seoul but picked up another plane the next morning. Each hour's delay seemed months long but my spirits rose as I looked down at my homeland and saw that it was verdant with new life after the rain. At last the fast plane trip—seemingly a long one to me—came to an end. We grounded at Kimpo Airfield where my good friends, Dr. and Mrs. Hugh H. Cynn, and their son Ted, along with Iris, met me and took me straight to the hospital. Lotus was in the Seventh Day Adventist Sanatorium outside the East Gate.

When I stepped into the room the sight of my pale, emaciated girl told me that death was near. Her voice was gone and she could only mouth words without a sound. She tried to say "Mother," but I could not hear any voice. I tried to compose myself and cheer her by telling her that I had brought the newest medicine, streptomycin, but she could not comprehend it. She closed her eyes and appeared to be almost dead. The love of a mother for her child is the strongest in the world, and how I wished that I could take her place. Alas, no one can take another's place in suffering or in death. As long as there is life there is hope so I went to see the doctor in charge, giving him the streptomycin which he immediately administered and gave directions for additional treatments every three hours.

Then I said to Lotus, "Let us give our full co-operation to the Chief Physician. When you pray, imagine yourself as well again; strong and healthy. I will do the same for you. Keep up your spirit!"

She began to rally and in three days I could see that the will to live had revived under the combined efforts of medicine and my presence with her.

There were seven other rooms besides Lotus' in that quarter of the hospital in which young men and women were dying of tuberculosis. I visited them one by one and found each filled with hope, which I understand is typical of patients suffering from this disease. One day a young man said, "As soon as I get well I will go to America for a good training in civil engineering so that I can help Korea in laying our future foundations for rebuilding." When I went to visit Lotus the next day I learned that he had died during the night. The girl who roomed next to Lotus had said to me, "I have no parents to care for me. I have no one to bring me medicines to save my life as you have done for your daughter." Then she sobbed. It broke my heart to see these young people still hopeful of cure, whose illness could have been prevented by proper food and living conditions.

For three weeks Iris and our kind friends and I put forth our best efforts to effect a recovery for Lotus. We did all we could to supply nourishing food. I spent all my waking hours at the hospital. Gradually her voice began to come back with her renewed strength and soon she was able to sit up for a few minutes at a time. At the end of the sixth week I took her home and put her in bed in a sunny room. I had learned to give her hypodermic injections myself and hired an intelligent old woman to wait on her. This old lady had just lost her married daughter of tuberculosis and she took great pity on Lotus and did her best to serve her. During my first four weeks at home there were eight deaths due to tuberculosis among the sons and daughters of friends of mine. Of course we kept such facts from Lotus' knowledge; she probably could not have endured the continuous shock.

Throughout October and November she showed daily improvement. One afternoon when I entered her room upon returning from a visit with a friend, I saw two persimmons on the table and asked, "Who brought the fruit to you?"

"I picked them from the branch hanging over the wall. Don't you see there were four, and now only two are left?"

She laughed with sheer joy that she was able to get up and pick them herself. Soon she was able to walk to the living room and often received the telephone messages when there was no one else about. My child was saved from near death! What a miraculous thing it was to witness the mending of her poor body.

During the ten months that I had been away from my

homeland great changes had taken place. Now the population was a mixture of all the people of all the provinces of my country; all classes of society had mixed, resulting in a homogeneous mass. The population of Seoul had increased to nearly one million. The local people had offered their spare rooms to house the newcomers from north of the 38th parallel and consequently there were few vacant rooms anywhere. Refugees from the Communist Zone started new Christian churches because the older churches were already filled with worshipers. The multitudes going to church on Sunday morning were really an inspiring sight. However, people in the stores and on the streets often presented pathetic pictures of poverty, although their determination to make their new-found freedom work was demonstrated in their endeavor to make themselves self-supporting. Everybody was eager to earn a living. It was often necessary to improvise implements in order to manufacture a certain article since machinery was scarce. Unbelievable obstacles were conquered under the pressure of necessity. And so once more such articles as bicycles, rubber shoes, bricks, utensils and textiles were produced.

Korean leaders had taken over the reins of government, having been trained by the Americans. The Military Government was preparing for the active functioning of the new Republic of Korea, writing the new constitution, and setting up the various departments of government. Factories were running and public utilities were operating under Korean leadership.

Many calls began to come from girls' schools and women's organizations in South Korea; people were eager to hear what I could tell them of the American people. I also visited the hospitals for American G. I.'s, taking them gifts and arranging entertainment for them under the auspices of the Patriotic Women's Society. I spoke to many groups of G. I.'s who were eager to have the latest word from home. These activities occupied me for four months while Lotus continued to improve. With her convalescence she became increasingly aware that my work had been brought almost to a standstill because of her, and so she urged me to think once more of returning to America and resuming from the point where I left off. Thus the matter was under consideration and discussion by family and friends.

The Soviet-American Joint Commission never completed its duties because Soviet Russia opposed every suggestion made by American leaders. There was frequent Communist sabotage of factories and schools, and bloodshed was common. The Russians were just as impossible a people to work with as the Japanese had been. In fact, murder was rife. The following is a case in fact: One day D. S. Chang, whom I had met in America and in England, was coming out of the Capitol as I was going in. We stopped to chat a while, and during our talk he said, "I hear you are soon returning to America. I wish that I could hide in your suitcase." The next day he was shot by the Communists. Naturally I called on his wife immediately upon learning the tragic news. His wife, Grace Pak, an American graduate, told me the circumstances surrounding his assassination. There had been no warning whatever. The family was just ready to sit down at the dinner table with a few friends when a stranger came to the gate and called him out. Walking out with a smile, Dr. Chang greeted the man and asked what he wanted. Without saying a word the man pulled out his revolver and shot him point-blank. Upon hearing the explosion those inside rushed out to find him already dead. The fact that he was still smiling when he died proved a mite of comfort to his wife. Many, many of Korea's leaders were purged in this manner. Tragedy stalked the streets.

I was surprised one day to be called into General Hodge's office. He asked me how my daughter was, expressing regret that I had been called home on such a sad errand, but glad that she was improving. Then he told me that I was needed to go to America on a Korean Cultural Mission, provided I felt that I could leave Lotus. He offered me his fullest co-operation if I could be financially responsible for the trip. He wanted me to present the situation of Korea to American audiences, to paint a true picture for them. We agreed that I was not to go as a government representative but rather as a free agent. This was a call I felt I must answer. When asked how soon I should be ready to go, he answered, "As soon as possible. Can you get ready in a couple of days?"

Again Lotus urged me to go as she was rapidly regaining her strength. Iris, who was now married and living with her husband's family according to custom, assured me that she could look after Lotus in my absence. She was expecting a baby and would be at home more than formerly. Whether I returned to America or worked in Korea it seemed that it might be best for Lotus to live with Iris for a time. The two girls were very companionable. Each would mean much to the other.

On December 6, 1947, three days after General Hodge had asked me to go to America, I left Kimpo Airport on a Northwest Airliner, again to follow the shortest route from the Orient to the United States. How proud I was to be chosen to serve my country on a cultural mission.

17

Cultural Mission

It was a gray dismal morning when I took off, but when we overrode the clouds the sun was there and our plane glided like a ship over the sunlit clouds. The ride to Tokyo was very rough; when the plane plummeted downward into an air pocket my physical heart sank with it but my spirit continued to soar because Lotus was on the road to recovery. After changing planes at Tokyo, I covered the return route to Anchorage, Alaska, and while getting my entry permit asked the officer in charge what time the sun rose and set at that time of the year. He told me it rose at ten and set about two in the afternoon. Too little sun for my nature.

From Anchorage we flew over Canada and the northern United States, and as I looked at the gray and white world below covered with snow and ice, it seemed that all the warmth of the world was sealed under an ice-covered mass. At dawn, I was struck by the positive power of the sun over the negative power of the icy forces enveloping the world and by the power of our airplane conquering space, and I said within my heart, "To man, with God, all things are possible."

We arrived at LaGuardia Airport at midnight on December

11, 1947, and I went to Ridgewood to my American home
with the Hardenberghs. Sending Christmas greetings to all
of my American friends was a joyful experience for something
new and lovely had come into my heart with Lotus' recovery.
Having her restored to me seemed a greater miracle of new
life than her birth had been. I was filled with the wonder
and promise of Christmas.

Christmas Day was spent with my friends, Mr. and Mrs.
Morton Snyder of Rye, New York. Mr. Snyder had been
headmaster of the Rye Country Day School for twenty-five
years. On Christmas Eve, while watching the fire in the fireplace, Mr. Snyder read aloud Dickens' *A Christmas Carol*,
and Kate Douglas Wiggin's *The Birds' Christmas Carol*. The
experience was altogether such an enjoyable one that I was
to spend other such Christmases in their home. That year
the beautiful Christmas dinner seemed fabulous after coming
from a war-stricken country where scores and scores of refugees were vainly hunting for food. The abundance in the
supermarkets also seemed overwhelming.

Mrs. H. M. LeSourd of Newton, Massachusetts, called me
to learn whether I could speak to her Boston Professional
Women's Club luncheon. It proved a special occasion for me
because I had the honor of presenting an award to Mrs.
LeSourd, who was president of the club at that time. She
had helped to organize Kappa Phi, a society made up of the
Methodist girls of state colleges and universities, and through
these channels had become a benefactor to Korean women
in general as well as to Ewha students in particular. Under
her enthusiastic spirit, aid had been sent to Korea innumerable times, supplying very definite articles, or financial help,
as the need arose. Before I left Korea the president of the

Patriotic Women's Society, Pak Seung-Ho, had brought me a beautifully carved white jade incense case to present to Mrs. LeSourd as a token of appreciation for what she had done for the women of Korea over the years.

Invitations now began to come from north, south, east and west. Due to the Korean political situation the American public had suddenly awakened to the fact that little Korea was fast becoming a crucial point in the Far East. I felt it my duty to make personal contacts and create friendships for my people. I was sure that Americans would be deeply interested in Korea when they understood the facts, for I know that "when they are interested, people care; when they care, they share."

In my lectures I like to portray my people by comparing the three great Far Eastern peoples—the Chinese, Japanese and Koreans. The Chinese, a continental people with over five thousand years of history, are stubborn, philosophical, rational, practical and industrious, and they have a keen sense of humor. On the other hand, the Japanese, an island people with some twenty-six hundred years of history, have a population of over eighty million crowded into small space and often subject to earthquakes and typhoons; they are a nervous, quick-moving, co-operative, progressive, aggressive and thrifty people. Also they are very artistic and delightful company socially. The Koreans, a peninsular people with over four thousand years of history, a population of thirty million, fall in between these two groups temperamentally and are neither stubborn like the Chinese nor nervous like the Japanese, but just a good medium. Climatically Korea is also in-between, having a combination of the Chinese continental climate and the Japanese marine climate, resulting in a healthy climate similar to the east coast of the United States from Maine to South Carolina, except that Korea has a rainy season during July and August. Each of these peoples has a characteristic pattern of dress, especially noticeable in the sleeves. Traditionally Chinese sleeves are long and narrow, Japanese sleeves are wide and loose, Korean sleeves are in-between, with a curved line, neither long and narrow nor wide and loose—just right! We three peoples use chopsticks for eating, and in these too a distinctive pattern obtains. Chinese chopsticks are long and blunt, Japanese chopsticks are short and sharp, and Korean chopsticks are in-between, neither long nor short, neither blunt nor sharp—just right! As to food preference, the Chinese eat a great deal of pork, the Japanese mostly fish, and we Koreans eat chiefly beef. We are better at walking than most other nationalities. Also we generally have splendid teeth. We use salt to cleanse teeth and mouth, rather than a candy-flavored toothpaste.

In art, the Chinese have perfected form; the Japanese have perfected color; and the Koreans have perfected line—curved and pleasing to the eye and expressed in everything, even in the thatched roofs of the houses. We say, "A straight line is a duty; a curved line is a beauty." Thus we, the Korean people, come in-between the Chinese and Japanese geographically, temperamentally and culturally. Therefore we are "happy middle-roaders and peace-loving"—never having been guilty of invading another country. Our love of peace is expressed even in our form of morning greeting to one another, "Did you sleep in peace last night?" We begin to talk of peace the minute we wake up, but at the same time I admit that this greeting exemplifies our tendency to look into the past rather than the future. In America the first greeting is "Good morning" whether the morning is fair or dull, indicating a look to the future. Our civilization looks backward and the other looks forward. To us Koreans, too, many unwritten laws have been handed down from generation to generation, dictating to the young, teaching them to accept and obey from the hour of birth so that an individual cannot overthrow the weight of the past by himself. Since liberation, however, the weight has been lifting rapidly, due to the mixing of the people.

The second point in my lectures about my country deals with the division made at the 38th parallel with the coming of the Allied Forces. Korea is a mountainous peninsula between the Yellow Sea on the west and the Sea of Japan on the east. It is separated from Manchuria and Soviet Russia by the Yalu and the Tuman Rivers, but it touches Siberia for eleven miles in the extreme northeast, only a hundred miles from Vladivostok. In the northwest a five-hundred-mile frontier lies along Southern Manchuria. To the south is the Strait of Korea studded with many islands, the largest of which is Chejudo (Quelpart). The area of my country is 85,246 square miles, slightly larger than the State of Utah, or the combined area of Belgium, The Netherlands, Luxemburg, Denmark, Switzerland and the Republic of Ireland. The coast line extends more than six thousand miles, with many seaports such as Rajin, Chongjun, Wonsan, Pohang, Pusan, Mokpo, Kunsan, Inchon, Chinnampo and Yongampo.

Many people have asked me in what ways the North Koreans are different from the South Koreans—as if we are two entirely different peoples. Until recent times we were one people under one government, using the same language and having the same culture. North and South are necessary to each other for North Korea has rich natural resources such as forests, coal, silver, gold, iron and other mineral ores, as well as abundant waterpower with power stations, while South Korea is mostly agricultural, and sends food, grain and manufactured products to the North. North and South have been interdependent for over four thousand years. If our country is cut in half it cannot function normally. With the present division, the people in South Korea have legs but no head, and in North Korea they have a head but no legs. If any living organism is cut it bleeds. Such is the case of Korea.

That line—the 38th parallel—is like a balance scale, with totalitarianism on one side and democracy on the other; whichever way the scale tips the fate of the East will be decided. Communism has made headway by stressing the fact that for centuries in Korea the ruling class has held supremacy over the common people and exploited them, that the proletariat will have to capture the political machinery if they want to get power, and to do so they will have to eliminate all the other classes by putting them in slave camps or killing them outright. There is no room in the Communist plan for any but the proletariat. Also a fundamental dogma of Communist ideology is collectivization of the land. In agricultural countries or areas where farm land is held in big estates, they promise to break up and distribute the holdings among the small people, but in industrial countries or communities they concentrate on the injustices and hardships experienced by the workers and thus create a state of agitation and unrest, holding out the promise that the workers shall have an equal share of production.

We Koreans now know that the Communists have worked out well-designed programs for each of their objectives. We recognize the five steps toward the achievement of their goal: (1) To make communism secure and strong in Russia, the home base of communism; (2) to soften other countries by infiltration, propaganda, subversion and fifth-column activities; (3) to create as many satellite countries as possible by sabotage, *coup d'etat* and civil strife; (4) to use the satellites as agents of Soviet aggression, without commitment of Russian manpower but with her material assistance and guidance; (5) to strike the home base of democracy a crippling blow— the United States of America! We have also felt the impact of a Communist-trained army.

To make the Communist threat graphic I catalogue Communists by degrees: There are the "red apple," the "tomato," and the "watermelon" Communists. The red apple Communists are red on the outside but white inside. These are the ones who have been forced to subscribe to Communist propaganda where the Communists are in power but they do not believe in it in their hearts. The masses are red apples, and are the least harmful. The tomato Communists are all red through and through, and are the thoroughly indoctrinated, Moscow-trained, firm believers in this ideology. Watermelon Communists are the ones who appear green on the outside but are red on the inside. These are the most dangerous, as they look harmless but are filled with deep red convictions. Often they are the underground workers. When people in an audience ask what we can do about them, I suggest that we make applesauce from the apples, tomato juice from the tomatoes, and pickles from the watermelon—and eat all of them up. In doing this we will need but two aids—

fire and sugar. The fire of enthusiasm and the sugar of love can change all. We just have to be fanatical for our own cause of democracy and world-wide brotherhood. The Chinese have a proverb, "Within the four seas all men are brothers." Jesus put it another way, "One is your father and all ye are brethren."

The last point of my lecture is to let the American audience realize the importance of educating Korean young people to do the democratic mission work. Had it not been for my American benefactors I would not have got my education. Most of the Korean men and women leaders of today in government, education, science, industry, agriculture, medicine and other important fields are the ones who received a Christian education. We are determined to steer our people to the democratic way of life and to make Korea a strong democratic nation in the Far East.

Several colleges and universities have responded to my appeal to educate tomorrow's leaders by providing full scholarships on which ten women and six men have already been brought to the United States. They are specializing in obstetrics and gynecology, architecture, music, science, engineering, primary education and dietetics. Altogether now there are about one thousand college and graduate students studying in the United States. Think what an investment that is for Korea!

Aside from bringing Korean students to America I have secured scholarships for eighteen boys and girls who go to high school and college in Korea. Eight of them have already finished. All these scholarships have been given by individual friends and church groups. I feel that I am a sort of telephone operator connecting parties. Or better still, I am the liaison officer between the eager-to-learn Korean youth and the willing-to-help American friends.

The time element involved on this cultural mission greatly exceeded that spent on any previous trip. Wherever I went, I always kept in mind that I was the symbol of the Korean people to all with whom I came in contact, and that my people would be judged through me. I have never had a really unpleasant experience during all of my travels.

I use the bus a great deal when there is sufficient time between engagements; when time is short I use the train; and when it is at a premium, of course I use a plane. I have always enjoyed watching people, and talking with them whenever possible. When the fat ones board a bus or train, they usually look about before selecting a seat, and finding a large part of my seat available because I am small and take up little space they sit down by me—sometimes almost hiding me from view. Invariably my seatmate opens the conversation; and such a friendly interchange makes travel in America different from that of any other country I have visited. I always wear my Korean garb, so naturally the conversation gravitates to the subject of my people and their problems. Thus I give many lectures to the people I meet, even as I journey along. Frequently also my fellow travelers drop gems of wisdom which I carefully record in my diary. Usually I am asked what my religion is, and when I say that I am a Christian the next question is likely to be about my denominational affiliation. One day when the conversation took this turn I stated briefly that I was a Methodist. The man who shared my seat told me that he was a Presbyterian. Then laughingly, he made the following comparison: "Each denomination has its strong point. The Methodists dig people out of the ditch, the Baptists wash them, the Presbyterians blue and starch them, and the Episcopalians polish them off." After enjoying our good laugh together, he concluded, "All co-operate to make a finished product."

A woman seatmate, who apparently thought I was a Japanese, once said to me, "I have read that seven Japanese babies are born every minute. This is a serious problem since Japan is already overpopulated. What are you going to do about it?"

With a grin, I replied, "What can I do about it? I am not a Japanese."

After thinking for a while the woman evidently decided that I must be a Chinese, for she said, "Is it true that every fourth baby born in the world is a Chinese?" When I replied in the affirmative, she continued, "What are you going to do about this?"

Once again stifling my amusement, I replied, "How can I do anything about it? I'm not Chinese; I am a Korean." At last, with my nationality established, the conversation turned to the Korean situation.

It has been a continuous source of amazement to all newly arrived Koreans to see how well Americans care for their children and what pains are taken for their safety and protection. When we see school buses loaded with happy children being given the right of way as they load and unload their precious cargo, sometimes with a long line of cars and trucks behind them waiting for the children to reach the safety zone before proceeding, we realize that America is indeed a child-centered country. This conviction is also deepened by the sight of boys and girls serving on the safety squads, directing other children crossing the streets near schools.

In the first three years of my cultural mission some very grave and important events took place in my personal life, as well as in the lives of my countrymen. In April, 1948, I received a cable from Lotus. It read: "CONGRATULATIONS MOTHER YOU HAVE BECOME GRANDMOTHER STOP IRIS GAVE BIRTH TO A BOY EARLY THIS MORNING." My first reaction was, "It's too bad the child wasn't a girl." Then I wondered what my father's reaction would have been to my reaction! But selfishly I had wanted a granddaughter who might grow up to graduate from Ewha also, and thus form the first grandmother-mother-daughter combination for this school. The birth month of the baby was the month of the dragon, a propitious sign for a boy. I wanted him to be worthy in every way, for the sake of his family as well as his country. It scarcely seemed possible that Iris, who was only five years old when I first came to America, was now a mother.

The following year the greatest sorrow of my life came quickly and unexpectedly. Lotus had an attack of virus pneumonia and she did not have enough stamina to resist it. Customarily she wrote to me every week—but for two weeks I did not hear from her. Then on March 5, 1949, I received a letter from Iris telling me of Lotus' sudden death ten days previous, and of her cremation. When this news came I was packed and ready to leave for four very important speaking engagements. Benumbed with shock, I felt that half of my body had been cut away. I wanted to cry aloud, "My God, my God, why has Thou forsaken me!" We Koreans have a saying, "When your parents die you feel as if your head is banged against a pillar; when your husband dies you feel as if the heavens fall on you; but when you lose a child, your heart aches." How true this is. In the death of one's parents or husband the pain comes from the outside in, but in the death of one's child, it starts from within.

I shall ever be grateful that when such tragic news came to me I was with my kind and good friends, Mrs. Hardenbergh and her dear mother, Mrs. Sunderland. Throughout Lotus' former illness Mrs. Hardenbergh had sent us ninety vials of streptomycin. Words are just not adequate to say what we feel toward her.

As I was forced to leave on my trip about fifteen minutes after having read my letter I did not have time to let down, and thoughts of my mother's strength of character sustained me for a time. I took the Upper Ridgewood bus to the terminal and changed to the Inter-city Line to New York, then on to Providence, Rhode Island. I sat in a seat away from the crowded section. Then the tears gushed out and I cried both for my mother and my child. When the conductor came for my ticket he saw that I was weeping and said, "Can I do anything for you?" The way he said it was too kind for words.

When I arrived in Providence two friends came and drove me to their home in Norton. All during the week that followed my faith was put to the test. "Sorrow comes to all but sours some." I was not going to let sorrow dominate my heart and make my whole life miserable. Instead I felt the "everlasting arms" supporting me, particularly in those days. Learning of my loss, friends from far and near sent me their expressions of sympathy. One, who had experienced grief, wrote: "We must not think of how unhappy we are in our loss, but rather how happy they are in their gain." This friend had lost her companion of thirty-five years, and had no one left. I still had one daughter and my new grandson, and felt that I was greatly blessed.

Between the birth of my grandson, Lee Joong-Hee, and the death of Lotus, the Republic of Korea had been born. The United Nations Temporary Commission arrived in Korea in January, 1948. After the Russian Government refused to co-operate, the plebescite was held in South Korea on May 10, at which time two hundred seats in the National Assembly were filled. Based upon population, one hundred seats were left to be filled by the North Korean voters, but the Assembly members from North Korea were never allowed to make their appearance. In July, the Assembly adopted a constitution, the first in its four thousand years of history, providing for the choice of a president by the National Assembly, and Syngman Rhee was chosen. He was inaugurated as President of the Republic of Korea on July 25, 1948. On August 15, the Republic was proclaimed by the ringing of an historical bell on Chongno (Bell Street) announcing the birth of the new Korea. The year 1948 was a prolific mother for on August 17, the Republic of Indonesia was born, and in May of the same year, the State of Israel had come into being.

All of these events were supervised by the United Nations without the co-operation of Russia. Although the new government was intended for all of Korea, lack of co-operation made it ineffective north of the 38th Parallel. In South Korea, in spite of this opposition, 91.3 per cent of the eligible voters registered; 94 per cent of the registered voters voted, and almost one-half of these were women. The enthusiasm of the women voters was touching. In many instances they appeared at the

polls early in the morning in order to be the first to cast their
ballots. One woman carried her invalid sister to the polls on her
back. The Korean W.C.T.U. urged General Hodge to
prohibit the sale of liquor during the election and he complied
with this request. On that first election day a magnificent page
in Korean history was written.

The National Assembly voted to ask the United States Army
to remain until the new government was reasonably secure, and
although most of the army was withdrawn in 1949 some five
hundred were left as a military advisory group. The American
Military Government ceased to function, and the United States
Department of State took over all of the responsibilities of the
army, with John J. Muccio as ambassador. The Economic
Co-operative Administration (E.C.A.) did a great deal in
guiding this infant government.

Land reform begun under the American Military Government was continued with provisions which made it easy for
Korean farmers to own small farms. Farm rentals were reduced
to 30 per cent of the principal crop for five years, after which
the land became the property of the tenant. Landowners were
reimbursed in national bonds in the same amount—150 per
cent of the value of one year's principal crop. At the same time
in North Korea under the Russian form of government, called
the People's Democratic Republic of Korea, not only did the
Communists fail to give the farmers title to their land, but
they took more than 50 per cent of the crops as taxes, and they
gave the best land to Communist party members. Under the
new Republic of Korea, public utilities, including water, rail-
roads and electric power, were operated by the government.
Mines and fisheries, developed with American aid, were also
under government supervision.

While this program was being carried out in South Korea, the Communists in North Korea were stretching their claws underground, as well as on the surface, in an effort to halt progress in the South. They even cut off the electric power upon which factories in the South depended. This, of course, put the people in darkness, and necessitated the local generation of electric power, a difficult undertaking since the water power was mostly in the North.

There were frequent skirmishes between the guards at the 38th parallel. Then suddenly, early in the morning of June 25, 1950, instead of skirmishes, there was a real invasion by a well-equipped North Korean Communist army, with Russian arms, tanks and planes. The U.S.S.R. had been training and equipping a large army ever since they arrived in North Korea, while in South Korea, although there was a constabulary to keep internal order, there was no army to defend the people from attack. In three days Seoul was in the hands of the Communist army. The Communist war had started in Korea.

I had been planning to return to Korea that summer and had made plans to fly on a Northwest Airliner from Seattle on July 1. On my way West I stopped to visit some friends in Detroit. On Saturday, June 24, Mr. and Mrs. Y. P. Jhung and Dr. and Mrs. Matthew L. Simpson and I were driving in the Jhung car when we heard over the radio the startling news that the Communists had crossed the 38th parallel with an army.

Since government officials, political leaders, ministers, teachers and notables were the first to be liquidated, it certainly would not be wise for me to rush headlong into the trouble. While speculating as to what my next step should be, I recalled a vivid and dramatic dream in which I was walking alone along a lonely road at dusk when a huge lion dashed into my path.

My scream of terror was at the same time an appeal to God for help! The lion was crouching and approaching me with snarling mouth. All of a sudden I saw that two strong arms were extended over my shoulders from behind, and two powerful hands seized the lion's two front paws and pulled backward, pinning me between the lion and the unseen one. In an effort to do what I could to help, I grabbed the lion's throat between my two hands and pressed upon the jugular vein until it was punctured and the animal's blood spurted from his throat. Finally he fell dead. When I looked back of me the unseen helper was gone. I had never felt so mighty as I had in that dream. I had killed a lion! And the more I thought about it the more certain I was that this dream contained a clear warning for my 1950 conduct. As my mother would say, there is no point of "dashing into fire carrying gunpowder, or plunging into water with a bag of salt." I decided to move slowly.

18

Cultural Mission Continued

Weighing all the factors I decided to go back to the east coast and wait until the North Korean aggression was halted. Surely this was just a display of Communist power, a bid for attention, an attempt to embarrass the highly successful democratic government of South Korea. Surely the Communists would not attempt to take the peaceful southern half of my country by force. My mind tried to reason that such cruelty could not be. Had my country become free from the Japanese only to be overridden by Russian force? No! Nevertheless, I knew the way of the Communists; honor, fair play, reason and truth were not a part of their equipment. Perhaps my family would be in danger because of my known American sympathy, my championship of democracy and my Christian convictions. If they were in danger I wished to share their peril. But if I returned to them, my presence might put them in greater danger. Hide though I might in some Korean mountain cave, I could not trust myself not to cry out against injustice and certainly I knew I could not stay hidden long when the people around me were in need. It was better that I stay where I was.

Each morning I rose with hopeful heart. Surely today the nightmare would be over. But instead the news from Korea got worse. President Truman ordered air and sea units to help South Korea. The United Nations Security Council called for U.N. members to give assistance to the infant Republic of Korea to expel the aggression, and asked the United States to appoint a commander for the U.N. forces in Korea. On July 8, 1950, Gen. Douglas MacArthur flew from Japan to Korea under the blue and white flag of the United Nations, carrying the flags of all the nations joining in the defense of South Korea. Thus Korea was the first country where the U.N. flag became a symbol of defense against aggression.

As I listened to the radio at the home of Mr. and Mrs. C. W. Crowell in Rochester, New York, a telephone call came from the Voice of America in New York, asking me to return to New York City as quickly as possible. I literally rushed back. I had been given a special assignment on their psychological warfare program, my commission being to prepare and give a thirteen-minute message of encouragement, cheer and inspiration to be broadcast to Korea once a week. The recording of my talk was broadcast at 6:45 Sunday mornings, which would be 8:45 Sunday evening, Korean time. I felt like a warrior going into battle for the sake of my daughter, my little grandson and my countrymen. To my people my message would be heartening, but to the Communists it must be word bullets. I realized that the enemy might try to do violence to my family in Korea because of my enlistment in the V.O.A., as the families, friends and relatives of the friends of America were the Communists' first targets in Korea. But this was a risk I must take, and Iris would want me to take.

All during July and August the war news became darker and more grim. Resistance and retreat continued until the R.O.K. and U.N. troops had been driven into a small perimeter around Pusan. Thousands had been captured and executed by the Communists and countless thousands of refugees had followed the U.N. forces back and forth. I had no idea what had happened to my daughter Iris and her family. Sometimes I felt such agony of uncertainty that I nearly screamed, and yet I felt that underneath the turmoil God was working a purpose out, that each of us must contribute his cup of courage to the common well from which humanity must drink. On September 15 the news was flashed forth that General MacArthur had directed the Inchon landings halfway up the peninsula one hundred miles behind the enemy. On September 26 the R.O.K. and U.N. troops recaptured Seoul. By October 20 the U.N. forces had a line well into North Korean territory, capturing Pyongyang, the Communist capital, and the enemy was in retreat.

With the U.N. victory, requests for speeches on Korea came thick and fast, as well as newspaper and radio interviews and magazine articles. I had to make two or three records ahead of schedule for the V.O.A. so that I could meet my speaking dates. I never had been so busy. On November 1 I had a speaking engagement at Haskell Indian School in Lawrence, Kansas. Half an hour before my appearance a pile of mail was handed to me, and the topmost letter had an A.P.O. postmark. Hurriedly opening it I found that it was from the son of my friends, Dr. and Mrs. La in Seoul. He wrote, "Your daughter and her family are missing." I felt as if I were falling into a bottomless pit. It was the first message I had had about Iris in over four months. After a little I turned to the second letter in the pile, which also had an A.P.O. postmark. I opened it and saw Iris' handwriting! I leaped for joy, and shouted within myself,

"She is alive!" It was a sensation like awakening from a horrible dream. First I had lost her, then I had found her!

Iris said that she and her little boy were all right but that her husband was missing. She described the dreadful three months after the Communists came to Seoul, telling how the bridge over the Han River had been destroyed in order to deter the enemy from moving southward, and how finally she had got across the river by ferry after waiting several days. She was then expecting another child but had walked forty-five miles to her husband's family home near Suwon, with a bundle of her possessions on her head and her two-year-old son holding her hand. There she had remained until the end of September when she heard of the Inchon landing and the recapture of Seoul and had walked the forty-five miles back to the capital. When she reached my home she found it occupied by refugees, and when she explained that this was her mother's home, they still refused to leave, saying that they had no other place to go. Putting herself in their predicament, she left them there and found a room elsewhere. In this room, on October 10, her second son was born. The date was the Chinese anniversary of the founding of the Republic of China. She wrote: "Mother, he is a victory baby, but we cannot call him Victory."

In Korea the boy babies' names are given by the father or the grandfather. Since the baby's father was missing, it was his paternal grandfather's responsibility to name him, but Iris had no way of contacting him except by walking the forty-five miles from Seoul to his home. So she suggested that I name the baby, saying, "I'm not going to walk that distance, ninety miles in all, just to have his grandfather name him." She also asked for a relief package of clothing, food and other necessities. This I sent as soon as possible, and then I began to think about a suitable name for my little grandson born in the midst of confusion and darkness. Realizing Korea's need for light I thought "Ray" would be a good name for him, and so for two months, the little fellow bore this typically American name. Finally I decided on Sun-Hee, to correspond with his brother's name, Joong-Hee. *"Sun"* means "good," and *"Hee"* means "bright" or "brilliant." I wanted him to be a good and brilliant boy.

Before Iris' baby was a month old the Chinese Communist "Volunteers," 200,000 of them, came into the war and General MacArthur ordered the U.N. troops north to the Yalu River, with a promise that the boys would be going home by Christmas. But Christmas found the Chinese pushing south, crossing the 38th parallel. Ever since Japan's surrender to China in 1945, the Nationalists and the Communists had been fighting over control of China and in 1949 the Communists dominated all China except for the island of Formosa, and proclaimed the People's Republic. Now the Chinese Red leaders threw their army into the Korean War, instilling their soldiers with a fanatical hatred of the "foreign imperialists," arousing them to sacrificial patriotism in a large-scale effort to win the war.

Ten days before Christmas Iris wrote to me: "Mother, Joong-Hee and Baby and I are leaving Seoul, heading for Pusan, following the refugees. If Ro Ui-Hyung [my uncle's grandson, a lieutenant colonel in the R. O. K. Army] comes to rescue us on the way, we will be lucky. It's pretty close to 300 miles to Pusan, and I have no idea where or how to get means to keep myself and the two children. I lost my gold ring and wrist watch when I left Seoul during the North Korean invasion so that I have no valuables to swap for food. But I am carrying a few pieces of silk, which I saved for such an emergency. The expected package from you has not yet arrived. I gave my cousin's address in Pusan to Sgt. H. L. Daniels, asking him if he would do what he could to have the package forwarded to that address, if it comes." She wrote again soon after she arrived in Pusan, saying that when she reached there she found twenty-seven relatives in her cousin's home, eleven of them under the age of eight with her baby the youngest of all. Pusan was a port town of about 400,000 before the invasion, now increased to two million. The greatest need was *water,* she said. She waited in line all night for her turn to draw a bucketful of water. On Christmas Day in the afternoon a strange G.I. had arrived with the hoped-for package which had been passed from one G.I. to another until it reached her. Said Iris, "I knew that the American G.I.'s were honest, but until now I never really knew *how* honest and helpful they are. What a wonderful Christmas gift that package was! With nothing of this world's good left, it was a real God-send."

I had tied the package with one continuous cord so that it could be used again, and as Iris untied knot after knot with the family crowded about her, little Joong-Hee danced about impatiently, crying, "Open it quick, Mommy. Cut it. Gaga [goodies], Mommy, hurry." He was remembering the delicious Honey Graham Crackers which I had sent in a previous package. Finally the box was opened and one by one the contents were removed and examined by all—clothing, soap, powdered milk, candy, cookies and mittens. Joong-Hee's Honey Graham Crackers were there and when he saw them he said happily, "Gaga, Mommy, gaga." A box of Charms was opened and solemnly passed from one to the other. Then someone said, "Let us ask grace," and after thanking God for His goodness, they all started to suck loudly on their candies to show their enjoyment.

Suddenly someone exclaimed, "Don't chew too loudly, the neighbors will hear you." Iris wrote, "We were all charmed by the Charms," and concluded by expressing the hope that Christmas might soon come to everyone in Korea, and all around the world, as it had come to them on that Christmas Day.

The Seoul Iris had left before Christmas had been lost to the Communist "Volunteers" and the North Korean Communists in early January, 1951, but by April the R. O. K. and U. N. forces had regained it. A minister friend in Korea summarized the whole situation in a nutshell: "In the seesaw war with the armies pushing back and forth, the damage done to our country is beyond any imagination or description. With the bombing and rebombing in attacking and counterattacking, the losses of life and property are beyond calculation. Homes are in ashes. There are millions homeless and hungry. Thousands are sick and dying. It's appalling, horrifying and terrifying! This is a living hell. What is the way out?"

Some of the Korean women decided to take up guns and help the men, so the Women's Military Corps, corresponding to the W. A. C. in the United States, was organized with a membership of twelve hundred under the leadership of Lt. Col. Kim Hyun-Sook, a former schoolteacher. Some of these women engaged in combat duty, but later they were withdrawn from the field and employed in administrative work.

On July 10, 1952, at the request of the North Korean Communists, coached by the Kremlin, truce talks were begun at Panmunjom. It took four months of negotiation to determine at what line hostilities would cease; then negotiations began regarding the exchange of prisoners, the withdrawal of troops, and other controversial issues. The firm and resolute stand taken by the United States and the United Nations regarding their principles and promises in respect to the prisoners-of-war issue will go down in history as one example of undaunted integrity, patience and persistence. From the time when the P. O. W. talks began until the signing of the truce, the shooting war continued, during which time the United States casualties mounted to 32,321, including 7,000 killed. Thousands of R. O. K. soldiers and hundreds more from the other fifteen nations died so that the 46,000 anti-Communist Chinese and North Korean prisoners could live. They died for their principles, individual freedom, the right to choose, to live and let live. In one week during the cease-fire talks, the Reds spent 159 minutes out of 187 for propaganda speeches. They spent 747 days out of the entire war period of 1,127 days just bickering, arguing, stalling, demanding more concessions in an all-out effort to wear down the democratic forces. But in the end they succumbed and the truce was signed on July 27, 1953, after 575 sessions of talking about a cease-fire.

Then the Neutral Nations Repatriation Commission was formed, made up of Sweden, Switzerland, Poland, Czechoslovakia and India, and the Communists tried to win over the anti-Communist Chinese and North Korean P. O. W.'s through "explanations," but only 3 per cent gave in while 97 per cent remained steadfast. The Reds had lost much face, which to an Oriental is unbearable. On January 21, 1954, the Repatriation Commission returned 21,513 anti-Communist Chinese and North Korean P. O. W.'s to their captors who freed them. Only 21 American war prisoners, one Briton and 325 South Koreans failed to return to their own countries. In this first war of the United Nations, the first jet-air war in history, the casualties were:

	Wounded or Missing	Dead
U. S. Forces	111,447	25,604
R. O. K. Forces	897,833	415,004
Other 15 Nations	14,076	3,184

In South Korea out of a population of 20,000,000:

2,000,000 died, including the R. O. K. soldiers
2,500,000 became homeless
5,000,000 depend in whole or in part upon relief.

Property destruction was incredible, while 75 per cent of the mines and the textile factories were out of action and two-thirds of the schools wrecked beyond repair.

In North Korea practically nothing was left. In a population of eight to ten million, one out of three died from war devastation or were purged by the Reds, besides the two million casualties of the Red Chinese and North Korean Communist armies. At the war's close the country once known as the Hermit Kingdom was bled white and still divided. But Korea is still half free and I believe that some plan will eventuate to speed up the liberation of the other half.

Under the rule of Korean monarchs and Japanese militarists the Korean people were not allowed to use their initiative. Therefore their creativity had no outlet. But now, under the leadership of President Syngman Rhee, any Korean who has a will to help the Republic can do so. There are pro's and con's about Dr. Rhee, but definitely he is the symbol of Korean unity, and is today the most hated man by the Korean Communists. Anyone hated so bitterly by the Communists is a good man for democratic Korea. His position is most difficult and we pray that his leadership and decisions will bring us through this most critical period.

Koreans are an agricultural people and their land has suffered. Hundreds of thousands of able-bodied young farmers were killed or maimed; a large share of the cows and oxen were casualties also. Therefore young war widows, children and old people have taken over the farming. In the place of an ox, four people are hitched to a plow and pull it through knee-deep mud to cultivate the rice. In 1953, in spite of such a handicap, we had the best crop in years. How thankful we are for the land, which is our most prized treasure. The land still remains after the war.

We have also our children, such as have survived the rigors of the war—3,000,000 elementary students, 400,000 high school students, and 50,000 teachers. In summer classes are conducted in the open air and in winter in damaged classrooms which have been fixed up by both teachers and students. How eager the young people are to learn, not only the three R's and the usual studies but also to learn how to build homes, schools, factories, and to operate machinery.

The interest in religion has also received new impetus. A new seminary has been opened at Taegu, with 500 students enrolled. These young men will be a powerful force for the spread of Christianity. Today there are at least two million Christians in South Korea, and so the potentiality for high morale under the stress of rebuilding and rehabilitating our country is very great. Christian social service is expanding. The Christian Lighthouse work, originally for the blind, now includes the deaf and dumb and amputees. There are four Lighthouses in South Korea, accommodating 139 persons; the members live in dormitories and are taught to farm and to work in factories. There is also a Braille publication for the use of the blind, of whom there are 40,000 in Korea today. Now the Association for the Chinese Blind in the United States and the American Foundation for the Overseas Blind, Inc. are giving them aid.

To my mind compassion has transformed the situation in our country from one of hopelessness to one of hope. We see consecrated and devoted workers tirelessly struggling against almost impossible situations trying to convert them into something productive. Hundreds of orphanages are being run on a shoestring. In a sense, Korea is but one big orphanage. Some G. I.'s and officers have been known to turn over all of their salaries for such work. For example, the Ranji-do Boys' Town was born last year, by the co-operative efforts of the Y. M. C. A. and The Fifth Regimental Combat Team. The members of the team donated first $1,800 to start Boys' Town; later, at Christmas, they gave $10,208.55 as "Operation Warmth." Boys' Town now has 200 orphan boys from eight to fifteen years of age in twelve different establishments. These boys grow their own vegetables and raise chickens and pigs on a one-acre tract of land. They have also a town hall, bank, barbershop, bathroom, outdoor theater, and a meadow for exercise and athletics. Certainly they are fortunate in their unfortunate situation. Boys' Town was dedicated to the memory of those members of the Fifth Regimental Combat Team who died in service. This is just one example of the way in which Koreans and Americans are united in compassionate service.

It seems to me that nearly everyone has done something for Korea, and people are continuing to sew for the babies, arranging for the adoption of Korean orphans via mail order, sending CARE packages, giving scholarships, organizing clothing drives. "Little drops of water, little grains of sand, make a mighty ocean . . ."

The Korean-American Cultural Foundation in Washington, D.C., of which my friend, Changsoon Kim, is the founder and president, is doing a splendid work in obtaining scholarships for the young people of Korea. Already the Foundation has brought nearly one hundred into the country, and many are on their way here. Quite a few of the first-comers have already returned to Korea and are active there. What a huge debt of gratitude my people owe to the greathearted people of America.

My personal life grows more interesting, more filled with adventure. In the fall of 1953, while I spoke for two weeks in Ohio, I made my headquarters with good friends by the name of Mr. and Mrs. J. B. McCarter of Crestline, Ohio. It was there in Crestline that I had my first lesson in driving an automobile. A Mr. Hutson, who teaches driving in the Crestline High School, was my instructor. One afternoon he took me out in his dual-controlled 1953 Chevrolet. The gear shifting came to me very easily, for I had practiced it mentally for three days, but the steering was just impossible. I had never driven even a bicycle or a horse and I had absolutely no sense along that line. I steered the car everywhere on the road but the proper place. On the second day I was turning the car around a curve when suddenly it jumped onto the sidewalk. My teacher said, "How did you do that?" I answered, "It was a miracle." But don't be alarmed if you should see me driving a car one of these days. What a joy and a pleasure it is to learn something new! When I was actually moving the car from behind the wheel, I felt as if I were just a college freshman. I learned swimming when I was twenty-eight years old, skating during my thirties, the Japanese language in my forties, and driving in my fifties. Now I am wondering what I should learn next.

Since the truce was signed, Iris has gone back to Seoul, living in my home which was greatly damaged. In fact, three families live there, each having fixed up one room. Iris has my picture on the wall. One day Joong-Hee, five years old, pointed to it and said, "Mommy, I know whose picture this is. Your mommy's, isn't it? I know where she is, too. She is in America. She is my hello-granny." To him, and many other children, hello means America. He asks a great many questions, such as How big is God? Why does the moon get larger and smaller? Why do the trains have to have tracks to run on? Iris writes me regularly about her boys in such detail that I feel as if I have a good visit with them each week. Joong-Hee has his mother's temperament, whereas Sun-Hee takes after his father. The oldest boy is a perfect "little man," cultured and refined in manner and appearance. The younger boy has a bubbling, radiant and "hail-fellow-well-met" personality. He calls all women of his mother's age "auntie," men of his father's age "uncle," and the older generation "grandfather" and "grandmother." It makes no difference whether or not he has met these people before. To him everybody is his friend. The children's father is still missing. And so Iris teaches music, going from home to home, to help support herself and the boys.

My mother-in-law, who had raised my girls and understood the stand which I had to take with regard to my marriage, died upon her return to Seoul. She had accepted Christianity several years before she died. My husband, who had been married twice since we were divorced, also died soon after the death of Lotus. Both had been so very sick that neither of them knew that the other had died. My youngest sister-in-law lost her husband; her daughter was graduated from Ewha College, and I am putting her son through college. Many of my good friends were killed by the Communists. But those of us who are still alive will live twice as hard and twice as fully because of the great amount of work to be done.

And so, this September Monkey hopes to go on traveling and speaking, renewing old friendships and making new acquaintances; sprinkling bits of love and encouragement here and there along the way; and opening up the ways of learning for Korean youth. When I was studying St. Paul's missionary journeys at the time of my imprisonment I too had a vision concerning my future work. So far, in four trips to America I have traveled 585,000 miles in thirty-five countries on four continents and eight islands in three oceans; I have flown 110 hours through the air and have given over three thousand speeches, mostly in North America. It is my hope to finish out one million miles. Most of my life has been spent in going places, but when I was *someplace* I was usually a guest in an American home. Hundreds of American homes have opened their doors to me, offering a most cordial and hospitable welcome. In many instances I have been made to feel as a part of the family, an associate member of a church or an honorary member of a club or society.

The great wish in my heart is to reopen Dukwha Institute on a different scale. I plan to make it a self-help school for boys and girls. Naturally, in speaking to nearly four hundred colleges, universities and vocational schools in the States, I have observed what type of educational systems would be adaptable to our situation. A learning center similar to Berea College in Berea, Kentucky, seems most ideal. Here the men and women students earn as they learn; they take liberal arts courses as well as practical subjects such as carpentry, furniture making, printing, dairying, horticulture, weaving, sewing, culinary arts and nursing. They also conduct a shop where articles made by students are sold. They have built some of their buildings as part of their study projects. They run their own hotel, acting as bellboys, clerks, cooks, waiters and waitresses. The college itself is a community where the students learn how to live happily and harmoniously with others from many states and overseas countries.

To me Berea College is such an inspiration that I have dreamed of naming my school "Little Berea in Korea." In undertaking such a program, securing well-trained teachers and funds for the building of such a village will be no small matter. But I am very rich in friends.

Today, my people as a whole have faced difficulties as my mother did; we are hopeful and resourceful and industrious. Above all, we have faith in our own abilities, in the free peoples of the world and in our God. Is it too much to hope that from the ashes of countless thousands of burned homes, the loss of hundreds of thousands of lives, there will arise a spirit indomitable, incorruptible, against which nothing of evil will prevail? Who knows, perhaps Korea is kindling the glorious flame which will bring light to the dark places of the world and the warmth of brotherhood into the councils of nations.

Appendix

All over the world people seem to have an interest in the development of their own personality. They like to know their own strong points and weak points; they want to understand how they became the sort of person they are. Even more, they want to know what they should do to become the kind of person they wish to be. They also have a natural curiosity to understand other members of their family and their friends. All young people want to marry the right partner, to assure lasting compatibility and a peaceful home life.

From the earliest times people have concerned themselves with the influence of the stars and planets, not only upon the seasons and the tides, but upon their own moods and vitality. Even upon their characters. And so every ancient culture has developed astrological insight, and invented a zodiac which charts the apparent influence of the heavenly bodies. Often the symbols of the zodiac are animals.

Such is the case in Korea. We have an ancient zodiac comprised of twelve animal signs which represent twelve years in rotation, twelve months of the year, twelve days of the month in rotation, twelve hours of the day as reckoned by the lunar calendar, which is the same as twenty-four hours of the solar calendar. The lunar calendar of hours starts at midnight and each hour spans two solar hours, so that the first zodiacal hour is from midnight to two A.M., the second from two to four, and so on.

By knowing the animal signs of the year, month, day and hour under which a child is born, and by recalling the characteristics of these animals, one may draw a rather accurate idea of the type of personality the child will have. One can hazard a fairly accurate guess as to the way in which this child will meet his problems, choose his friends, carry his responsibilities. One may prognosticate his dominant temperament, whether he will be lighthearted, morose, friendly or in-turned. To be sure, a child's environment will also condition his response to life, but the pattern of his response to environmental factors appears to be born in him.

Now we Orientals feel that when an individual approaches a significant event, such as his marriage or his choice of a profession, it is a good thing to take into account the personality pattern of the partner also. Thus the family from time immemorial has also looked at the animal signs governing the other person's life. Many modern young people, in throwing off the ancient customs, have also scorned these ancient insights. But the zodiacal chart has a great deal of folk wisdom behind it, and even the most up-to-date student is often astounded at the accuracy of the information it may offer him. If the insight had not proven relevant to human affairs it would not have persisted for thousands of years.

Not only do the signs have meaning, but also the seasons in their relationship to the signs. For instance, man's life is divided into four parts corresponding to the four seasons of the year—spring representing childhood; summer, young adulthood; autumn, middle age; winter, old age. But one's childhood starts in the season he is born. Thus if an individual is born in the autumn, his childhood and adolescence will portray the characteristics of his animals in that season—the animals dominating his year and hour being the most important. For instance, if he is born in the year of the tiger in the autumn, he is a fall tiger. In his young adulthood he will act like a winter tiger, in his middle years like a spring tiger, and in his old age like a summer tiger.

Of course an individual always has free will to make of his potentialities as much as he can. And if he is a Christian who has learned to lay hold on God's power, he can overcome his natural weaknesses and add to his natural strengths. He can also do the same for others. Nevertheless he has a basic pattern of personality, and knowledge of this inborn pattern may help him to plan wisely.

The following is the interpretation of the twelve animals, from which one may figure out his own birthday horoscope.

1. OX or COW. Mankind simply cannot get along without cows, and no part of the cow is wasted. Food, such as milk and meat, leather goods made from the hide, glue from the hoofs, and even the manure is utilized, making the cow indispensable. In Korea these animals are also used as beasts of burden. So it is with the people born under the sign of the Ox; they are very dependable, complacent, seemingly relaxed and unhurried, yet constantly doing something for humanity. All of society depends on them. All seasons are good for cows, although spring, summer and fall are their best, for then they can be outside grazing on the grass and clover. However, winter is also a productive season for the cows, with plenty to eat the year round.

2. TIGER. We Koreans call the tiger "king of all beasts," representing physical power with dignity and fighting force. Standing on a rock in the mountains, the tiger is a creature of beauty with its striped tawny fur, strong teeth and lashing tail, especially in a winter setting of white snow and tall green pines. Persons born under the sign of the tiger will have power, and people will love to look at them and yet fear them. We say, "The child is going to be great because he is born under the tiger sign." We must not forget that tigers, powerful as they are, have dangerous enemies in the hunters. Tiger fur, which is expensive, is used mainly by royalty and the wealthy class. Since the tiger is protected by foliage in the spring, summer and fall, these three seasons are best for him, with fall the most safe, since fall colors are most nearly like the tiger's coloring.

3. RABBIT. Since rabbits are so prolific, the first thing we think about rabbit people is that they will have large families. Next, because rabbits spend their time jumping about, we say, "You will always be busy." Remembering that children love rabbits because they are so soft and gentle, a person born under this sign is very successful with children. Rabbit meat is a delicious food, and rabbit fur is used for coats, trimmings and linings. So, as the rabbit is useful to humanity in many ways, we love to have rabbit people near us.

4. DRAGON. This is the only one of the twelve animals which is legendary, and although we have never seen a dragon we have some definite ideas as to its characteristics. We think of dragons as having magical powers, with great cunning and planning ability; that they can create storms—rain or wind—and that they can change an insignificant thing to a great thing, overpowering all. Although the dragon is not seen, he is often heard, and according to our interpretation the dragon is the greatest of all animals. So, a boy born under this sign may make history by becoming prime minister or a great leader. Dragon people can be chief executives, presidents of companies, kings, rulers, emissaries, or other such important dignitaries. Because we usually have many storms in the summer, and dragons have the power to change the summer sunshine to storm, we consider summer the dragon's best season. We think that when winter comes dragon people lose their magical powers, and that is good, for if the dragon had luck all year around, others would have no chance.

5. SERPENT. The serpent is generally spoken of as very wise, and we think of wisdom as the outstanding characteristic of this animal. So we say of a girl born under this sign, "She will supply all wisdom to her husband." Serpents, or snakes, do more for mankind than we realize, by eating insects, rodents, et cetera, and so people born under this sign render service to mankind—often without recognition. Spring, summer and fall are the best seasons for these animals, and they spend their winters in hibernation in cold climates.

6. HORSE. Whether a work horse or race horse, we find this animal good looking, strong, hard working, obedient and trainable. We say that a person having these same traits has "horse sense." The horse is useful in many ways for both work and pleasure, and its meat and hide are also made use of. In the spring, summer and fall the horse enjoys the freedom of the out of doors, and so we deem these three seasons best for horses and horse people.

7. SHEEP. This is the animal which during the ages has represented sacrifice. We must have people in the world who have the spirit of sacrifice for others, and people born under this sign have this spirit. Sheep also show a spirit of meekness, which has led to the saying "as meek as a lamb." These animals are useful in many ways, providing both meat for food and wool for clothing. Spring, summer and fall are their best seasons, although winter is not too difficult for them as they have such a thick covering to keep them warm.

8. MONKEY. Monkeys are notorious for their funny faces and funny ways, providing entertainment for old and young, regardless of age or sex. Whether born in the year, month, day or hour of the monkey, people born under this sign just cannot get away from entertaining people. Actors, actresses, acrobats and other entertainers are most frequently born under this sign. These people are very important in this world, as we must have people who can make the world laugh.

9. COCK or ROOSTER. This animal is considered to have a keen sense of time, frequently serving as time clock for farmers in the villages of Korea. The rooster is also a very busy animal, always scratching for something to eat; proudly he preens his feathers and shows a fighting spirit. So, people born under this sign show a fine sense of timing which manifests itself in pioneer work of various kinds. They are also very busy, proud and often belligerent. All seasons of the year are good for roosters except winter.

10. DOG. The various kinds of dogs are outstanding for their many characteristics which make them useful for racing, hunting,

guarding, guiding their blind masters, or as family pets. They are beautiful, affectionate, intelligent, watchful, faithful, loyal and companionable. People of this sign show these same traits.

11. BOAR. In our plain language we call a boar a pig. Here is an animal which gives of itself completely—meat, hide and bristles. As with the cow and oxen, all parts are made use of, and there is a saying, "All parts of the pig are used except the squeal." Pigs have good dispositions, except for a bit of grumbling now and then, and so it is with the people born under this sign. All the year round is good for pigs, and any season of the year is the lucky season for hog people.

12. RAT. Since the rat works diligently to store up food for winter, we say that persons born in the fall or winter in the year of the rat will be blessed with wealth, providing they are diligent and resourceful. They can accumulate great wealth if they are aggressive and progressive. On the other hand, the spring rat is lean and poor until after the spring and summer crops have supplied him with plenty of food. So we say that persons born in spring in the year of the rat will not be able to accumulate riches until later in life.

When the marriage of two persons is proposed, the families consider carefully their ancestry, personality and ability to care for a family, but they also never fail to look into the animal signs for both the bride and groom. If he was born under the sign of the tiger and she under the sign of the hog, we consider this a perfect combination, because the stronger animal absorbs the weaker. If the bride was born under a stronger animal than the groom, we say, "He is going to be a hen-pecked husband." By studying their animal signs, we have a good idea as to whether the couple will have a peaceful, harmonious life, or one of family strife.

To find the animal signs for recent years, one can begin with 1937, which was the year of the Ox, or Cow, and count the years in cycles of twelve, to 1949, which is again the year of the cow. Those who were born before 1937, may count the twelve years in reverse order, i.e. Rat (1936), Pig (1935), Dog (1934), et cetera.

To find the signs for the days, reckon from January 1, 1937, which was the day of the Ox. Those who were born before this day may count the twelve animal signs in reverse order, starting with Rat (December 31, 1936). Those who were born since January 1, 1937, may reckon ahead, starting with Tiger (January 2, 1937), et cetera.

To find the signs for the hours, one can begin with the hours 2:00 to 4.00 A.M., which is the hour of the Cow, and count every two hours through the twelve-animal cycle.

The animal signs for 12 months, 12 years beginning with 1937 and 12 hours (lunar calendar) are as follows:

CHART SHOWING THE TWELVE SIGNS

January	Ox	1937	2–4 A.M.
February	Tiger	1938	4–6 A.M.
March	Rabbit	1939	6–8 A.M.
April	Dragon	1940	8–10 A.M.
May	Serpent	1941	10–12 M.
June	Horse	1942	12–2 P.M.
July	Sheep	1943	2–4 P.M.
August	Monkey	1944	4–6 P.M.
September	Rooster	1945	6–8 P.M.
October	Dog	1946	8–10 P.M.
November	Pig	1947	10–12 P.M.
December	Rat	1948	12–2 A.M.

Set in Linotype Granjon
Format by Thomas Geismar
Manufactured by The Haddon Craftsmen, Inc.
Published by HARPER & BROTHERS, *New York*